Reconciling

Reconciling

John Coventry SJ

SCM PRESS LTD

334 022940

First published 1985
by SCM Press Ltd
26–30 Tottenham Road, London N1

Typeset at The Spartan Press Ltd
Printed and bound in Great Britain at
The Camelot Press Ltd, Southampton

Contents

Preface

The publication of this short collection in the spring of 1985 marks a turning point in my own life in arithmetical and other ways. Things come together when you can look back on seventy years of growing with the delighted realization that you can keep learning how to live, how to enjoy the gift of life up to any age. Things come together in a certain simplicity: the one word of the title (II Cor 5.14) is a symbol for the simplicity of the message.

I am not an academic theologian in any serious sense: I have lived with them and know the difference. But I have done my best to keep up with what scholars are saying in New Testament studies, systematic theology and philosophy of religion, as well as with the immense struggle towards Christian unity among the English churches. And so I may perhaps without too much conceit offer a message to the scholars too and hope that they may read this slender book. Morna Hooker wrote in the collection of essays published in honour of Christopher Evans that New Testament scholars are in danger of making New Testament authors in their own image and likeness – men piecing ideas variously together from their comprehensive libraries and painstaking card-indexes. What I would venture to add (as I have written in *Faith in Jesus Christ*) is that scholars seem to overlook the fact that after Easter Jesus' disciples *experienced* most vividly the living presence and continuing action of their Risen Lord among them, and that this was the matrix of all their theologies. There is good reason to hope that we may still be able to do that today, and relate all our thinking to our awareness of the Lord's gift of his Spirit to us all – i.e. to our experience.

I have just read Peter Hebblethwaite's admirable book on Pope John XXIII. The message that comes over most vividly to me in the course of this fascinating historical study, is how comprehensively out of touch the Vatican curial machine has been, from the beginning of the story about 1880 until its end (I may be oversimplifying somewhat) with all the real needs of the church and the world, and how John, not himself part of the machine, achieved so much for the church and the world by the sheer force of his holiness, goodness, reconciling power. If only all who follow Christ, at any 'level' in his community (communities), could confidently and joyfully use the freedom that God so urgently gives us in Christ, how much we could all advance his kingdom, how many obstacles difficulties hesitations hang-ups would simply vanish as the sun broke through!

One can but try.

Some of these chapters have appeared just as they are here, or in an earlier form, in different periodicals. I would like to thank the editors of the following periodicals for their permission to reproduce the material: 'Anglican Orders', *The Tablet*; 'Theology of Ministry', *The Sower*; 'Interchurch Marriages', *The Way*; 'Spiritual Health', *Catholic Medical Quarterly*; 'Theology of Sin', *The Way*.

I would also like to express my warm and deep thanks to the Fellows and other members of St Edmund's House, Cambridge, who housed, fed, supported and stimulated me as their Master during the years when I put these thoughts together.

November 1984
St Edmund's House, Cambridge   John Coventry S J

PART I

RECONCILING MAN WITH MAN

I

ANGLICAN ORDERS

Church, baptism, eucharist

The question of Anglican orders, and indeed those of other Christian denominations, raises a large number of interlocking issues. A single chapter can only sketchily indicate certain central points on which rethinking has proved to be necessary. It is hoped that the ensuing paragraphs will show that it would be disastrous for well-intentioned Catholics or Anglicans to aim for the recognition by Rome of Anglican orders on the simple 'pedigree' principle, that all or most Anglican bishops have in their ancestry a bishop ordained in the apostolic succession as this has been historically recognized by Rome. For such a process assumes all kinds of theological requirements for a true Christian ministry which few theologians, Catholic or Anglican, would now uphold.

The broadest issue is that of ecclesiology, the theology of the church, which has been the greatest focus of theological thinking in this century. It has been amply shown that Vatican II uses a variety of ecclesiologies and that after the council the Catholic Church is living, not with a single theology of the church, able to provide neat answers to all questions, but with a pluralism in ecclesiology which illuminates different aspects of the mystery of the church.

One tendency in Vatican II is to speak as though the validity of ministry made a Christian community to be 'a church'. Hence the ancient Orthodox communities are unequivocally 'churches'. Yet, in a famous statement Paul VI spoke of 'the Anglican Church' and looked forward to the time 'when the

Roman Catholic Church . . . is able to embrace her ever beloved sister'. The many studies of the origins of Christian ministry appear to agree that Christ founded a-church-with-a-ministry, not a ministry with instructions to produce a church. Hence theologians would hesitate today to say that the fullness or soundness of ministry is what makes a Christian community to be 'a church', though they might argue that some churches are more or less so than others. So, if at some happy point in the future Rome were able to say to the Anglican Communion: 'Now at last we can recognize that your orders are valid, and that therefore you are a church', Anglicans would reply: 'Not at all: we are a church, and therefore our orders are valid'.

Another question is that of communion with the see of Rome. The Anglican-Roman Catholic International Commission (ARCIC) came down on the side of saying: 'Being in canonical communion with the Bishop of Rome is not among the necessary elements by which a Christian community is recognized as being a church'.[1] The Congregation for the Doctrine of the Faith took exception to this,[2] arguing that the papal office was a constitutive part of the very nature of the church as instituted by Christ. It would appear to follow that the Orthodox churches are not fully churches.

Evidently, some points need clearing up. However, what is perhaps more important than such particular issues is whether any other Christian family quite shares the Roman Catholic vision of the *catholica*.

A second broad issue is the direct connection between baptism and the eucharist. The validity or reality of Anglican and other Christian baptism is recognized. Nowhere in Vatican II is there any suggestion that those validly baptized outside the Roman Catholic Church are not fully, truly, really, incorporated into Christ: the wording is carefully chosen to avoid any such suggestion. The baptized community incorporated into Christ is the body of Christ. The eucharist is the celebration by the baptized community of what it is, the body of Christ. It is obviously right and proper that the celebration

[1] *Authority* II, n. 12.
[2] *The Tablet*, 15 May 1982.

of the eucharist should be safeguarded by accepted church rules, but is it theologically conceivable that the baptized community should be *unable* to celebrate the eucharist? We have to remember that there is no evidence from New Testament times about who could or could not preside at the eucharist.

Apostolic succession and 'validity'

Historical study has established that in early centuries bishops were considered as succeeding to sees, not to their predecessors. Appeal was certainly made to lines of bishops supposedly going back to the apostles, but this is an appeal to recognized continuity in the apostolic faith and does not imply the idea of a transmission of power from bishop to bishop.

Apostolic succession has been treated by the Catholic tradition simply in terms of the outward sign, namely continuity in valid (recognized) episcopal ordination, a view dubbed by Professor Mascall 'the episcopal relay race'. The Reformed tradition has looked rather to the inner reality, namely continuity in the apostolic faith and life, but has not produced any clear criteria for such continuance. In the interchurch dialogues it has been recognized that apostolic succession must be understood as a combination of both factors, and cannot be reduced to one or the other. ARCIC stresses the fact that a number of bishops join together in the consecration of a new bishop.[3] This signifies the entry of the new bishop into a college of bishops which itself assures the continuing communion of the churches in the apostolic faith, life and mission. However, this raises a problem about the eastern churches. If valid episcopal consecration alone secures apostolic succession then both Orthodox and 'heretical' eastern churches have apostolic succession. If it is the college of bishops which secures apostolic succession, then how is the college defined? If it is defined as those in communion with Rome, then this excludes the Orthodox churches from apostolic succession.

It is not entirely clear what the word 'valid' means. It is of

[3] *Ministry and Ordination*, n. 16.

the nature of a sacrament that it embodies and assures the
grace of God. So, if church authority declares a sacrament
valid, it assures us that it conveys God's gift; but not that
God's gift can only be conveyed this way, or that God only acts
through authenticated sacraments. If the church withholds its
assurance, it leaves the matter in doubt. It is surely beyond the
power of church authority to give a guarantee that a sacramental action is *ineffective* and that God does not give grace.
The matter needs to be thought out fully in terms of baptism,
sacramental absolution, the eucharist, ordination and marriage.

It has been noted that in many places the ARCIC's
statements describe what is done in the two churches, rather
than prescribe what must be done. The commission was aware
that the threefold ministry took time to develop and to become
universal, and that there are no grounds for tracing later rules
about orders, or ordination, or eucharistic celebrants, in a
direct or simple linear way back to Jesus or his disciples.
Certainly, a right ordering of ministry and of sacraments is
necessary; and forms which developed because they embodied
great Christian values, and which endured unchallenged for
centuries, can be said to have developed under the guidance of
the Holy Spirit. But can what was not considered essential in
New Testament times for ministry or ordination thereby
become so absolutely necessary that no other ways remain
possible? Some of the Reformers were convinced that the
Spirit was guiding the church back in their day into what they
thought to be the primitive forms of ministry.

'Apostolicae Curae'

What is the status of *Apostolicae Curae*, the papal document
by which in 1896 Leo XIII declared that Anglican orders were
invalid? Professor Piet Fransen of Louvain has argued that the
decision was prudential and juridical, made in the light of the
theology of the time.[4] It has long been the teaching of moral
theologians and the practice of the Vatican that, in matters

[4]P. Fransen in *Church Membership and Intercommunion*, Darton,
Longman and Todd 1973.

concerning the validity of the sacraments, the safer or more probable opinion must be followed. *Apostolicae Curae* would fit into that category of documents: Rome did not see clear grounds at the time for reversing previous decisions about Anglican orders.

The argument of *Apostolicae Curae* centres on the Edwardine Ordinal, the Anglican ordination rite published during the reign of Edward VI. One has to recall that minimum, not maximum, requirements are necessary for the validity of sacraments; that heresy on the part of the minister does not make a sacrament invalid; and that an ordinal is not expected to express an adequate theology of ministry. Since Pius XII the 'essential form' of the Roman rite of ordination has been simply the laying on of hands by the bishop with the accompanying prayer. We do not know what forms of words were used in New Testament times. *Prima facie*, then, the Edwardine Ordinal is a valid form.

The argument of *Apostolicae Curae* involves the following steps: the essence of the ministry is sacrificing priesthood; the framers and users of the Edwardine Ordinal, as is clear from the Preface, altered previous models precisely so as to exclude both the idea that the mass is a sacrifice and the intention of ordaining priests. Their obvious and in itself sufficient intention of ordaining Christian ministers was cancelled out by their intention not to ordain sacrificing priests; hence defect of intention is manifested by the context of the Ordinal's devising and use; hence their ordinations did not transmit the powers of the episcopacy or of the priesthood. The Ordinal was subsequently changed and Anglican theology became broader, but the link had been broken and the ability to transmit priestly powers had been lost. This argument requires some comment.

(*a*) The theology of ministry has developed considerably since 1896. The ordained ministry is understood much more broadly as mediating the whole ministry of Christ. And while the mass is certainly understood as a sacrifice, the eucharistic ministry is itself seen more broadly as celebrating the whole communion of the members of the body of Christ with their Lord and with each other. Theologians would now hesitate to say that the essence of the ministry is sacrificing priesthood.

(*b*) The doctrine of conflicting intentions – that a wrong

intention about the heart of the matter can vitiate a more broadly valid intention – was never more than a theological opinion: but it was reasonable to espouse it in a 'play-safe' policy over the validity of sacraments, given the assumptions of the time. However, it remains questionable whether it is possible to determine the subjective intention of ordaining ministers from a historical study of the origins of a particular ordinal.

(*c*) The underlying idea that ordaining ministers transmit priestly powers, which they themselves possess, has been seriously questioned. It suggests too much that everything is handed over by Christ to the leaders of the church, and that they pass on the action of the Lord to others. It suggests too much that the church replaces Christ; too little, that his ministry and lordship continue and that the church can only mediate his continuing and active ministry. There are various factors in ordination which need interrelating: sacred power, which is the gift of the Spirit; the recognition by the church of God's gift and its incorporation into the official ministry; appointment to a particular responsibility, with the authority that goes with such responsibility; popular choice, which was a strong feature of appointment in early centuries, and can be thought of as giving rise to the role of leadership.

A great deal of theological work on the ministry has been published in recent decades, both by Catholics since Vatican II and by other Christians seeking to reconcile churches and ministries. The danger is that it all becomes too complicated. What is required is, not simply what Catholics and Anglicans can agree to be their common heritage, but an agreement on essentials with an eye to other Christian churches.

2

THEOLOGY OF MINISTRY

The theology of Christian ministry is essentially very simple. It can be set down in comparatively few words. But then mountains of words are needed to clear the ground and to allow it to operate freely.

I came to this conclusion after struggling with a fair part of the mountain of words (the literature that has been published on the subject in the last twenty years is massive), and after wrestling in the company of many other representatives of churches with many hours, weeks, months, even years of negotiations for unity, which all appeared to end in failure. Such negotiations for unity do not talk about God or his self-gift and self-revelation in Jesus Christ; they do not talk about the doctrine of creation, or of atonement, or of the sacraments (very much), or of grace. That ground has really all been covered. They talk about the ministry; about the clergy. And it is the clergy who are unable to accept the agreements when it comes to the crunch. Anglican-Roman Catholic unity is hung up about the ministry, what it means, what are its correct forms, where it truly exists. The Anglican-Methodist scheme of unity broke down on the reconciliation of ministries. And since the Proposals for a Covenant failed to gain acceptance from the House of Clergy in 1982 there has been a feeling all round that the sixty years of effort since the Lambeth appeal of 1920 has ground to a halt. The only success in the British Isles has been the union of the Congregational Church and the English Presbyterians in 1972, which later gathered to itself most of the Churches of Christ. Everything else imaginable seemed to have been tried. There must, I felt, be a new

approach, a way out somewhere. And then, into this darkness
there came a ray of light from another quarter.

Theology of faith

It can happen that systematic theology makes a great advance
in one area and that a considerable time elapses before other
areas catch up. One example appears in this book in the
chapter on interchurch marriages. For a very long time in the
Catholic tradition holy communion had been considered in
wholly individualistic terms as personal nourishment for 'my
spiritual life'. Vatican II's *Constitution on the Liturgy* in its
theology and in its practical reforms regained the ancient
understanding of the corporate and communal nature of the
eucharist. And yet the *Decree on Ecumenism* and the various
instructions that flowed from it, when treating the question of
eucharistic sharing, are still relying on the individualistic
understanding of the graces to be obtained: only the serious
spiritual need of the isolated individual is taken into account,
and not the spiritual needs of families, communities and
churches.

One of the great and in many ways revolutionary con-
stitutions of Vatican II was that on *Divine Revelation*, for
one of the areas in which great strides had been made was in
fundamental theology in general, and in the theology of
faith in particular. Views which were suppressed in 1951
emerged with the council's blessing in 1965 and could then
be freely published. I have treated the subject in three
semi-popular books[1] and can only give the briefest summary
here.

In systematic theology in the Catholic tradition, during the
post- or counter-Reformation period ended by Vatican II,
there prevailed a 'propositional' theory of faith. Faith was in
doctrines, in the teaching of the church; an assent of the mind
impelled by the will. Doctrines of the church, if defined, were
'of faith'. At Vatican II a long theological development broke
through into general awareness and acceptance. It consisted in

---

[1]*Faith Seeks Understanding*, 1951, suppressed; *The Theology of Faith*,
Mercier Press 1968; *Christian Truth*, Darton, Longman and Todd 1975.

going behind or beneath the level of statements to the personal relation of God and man. Revelation is not basically God giving information about himself (and about man) in scripture or in accepted tradition or in the teachings of the church based on these, but God giving himself, God addressing man personally and communicating his own self and being. Correspondingly, faith is not primarily an assent to revealed truths or propositions, but a recognition of God in his self-communication and a personal response, or response of the whole person. Of course, one then has to tackle the question of the necessary involvement of picturings, ideas, and their articulation in words, in the very act of man's recognizing and in his free self-giving and response. God is only grasped and responded to *in* the very act of articulating how I grasp him, so that revelation (God's act), faith (my recognition and response), and beliefs (my articulation of this recognizing) glide into and involve one another. But each *is* not simply the others.

The upshot is that, for a Christian, faith is always a grasp of, a recognition of and response to, God the Father as he reveals himself in his Son by the power of his Spirit. Faith is in Christ, as I meet and encounter him, not primarily in the pages of scripture but where he now is, now lives and acts, in his body the church.[2] Statements 'of faith' must be statements about Christ the Lord.

The moment you apply this to the theology of Christian ministry, you see at once that you need to distinguish two levels of statement. They are both theological in a broad sense. But only the basic statements about Christ can be 'of faith' and are *theo*-logical in the older and stricter sense. The second level of statement, depending on the first, needs some different designation. Let us say that they are value-statements and enunciate profound and tried Christian 'values' that come out of the historical experience of the Christian churches in many ages and situations. The church is a historical and changing reality, and from the day of Pentecost onwards has entered into and responded to new situations, met new challenges, in the attempt to fulfil its mission. What engages our *faith* is that Christ is encountered in the continually developing ministries

[2]See *Christian Truth* and also my *Faith in Jesus Christ*, Darton, Longman and Todd 1980.

of the church. But the *forms* of Christian ministry, the forms in which Christ is encountered, necessarily vary throughout the church's experience in different times and places, and will continue to vary. It cannot be said of any of these forms that Christ does only act, can only act, through them, great though their values have been for their times and places. It cannot be said of any of them that they are 'of faith'.

Theology of ministries

So, as was said at the outset, the theology of ministry is essentially very simple. It can be enunciated in comparatively few statements, even if many words have to follow to explain and to clear the ground. Such basic statements *of faith* must as far as possible be timelessly true and phrased in historically and culturally unconditioned language. They are not about particular ministries, all of which are historically conditioned, but about Christian ministry. They attempt to state what is essential about it whatever forms it takes. I offer three of them, though no doubt further discussion could improve on these.

1. *All ministries in the church serve and mediate the continuing ministry of Christ the Lord.*

Christ is constituted Lord in his resurrection (ascension, exaltation, glorification) and is present in our history and manifested in the community of believers by the power of the Spirit which he now shares with the Father and communicates to us.

He ministers in the church, his body. *He* sanctifies, *he* teaches, *he* governs, *he* inspires, *he* binds in unity, *he* sends us out to build the kingdom. Only a theological climate which had pushed Christ right up into heaven and made him absent from the earth (and filled the huge intervening space with mediators), by forgetting the patristic theology of the body of Christ, could begin to talk about the ministers of the church from the apostles onwards as 'taking the place' of Christ, as if he were an absent Lord who guided his church in history from afar or had left a human organization 'in his place'. No one takes his place. In a basic and profoundly important sense there are no vicars of Christ, no substitutes (*vicarii*) for Christ.

For he is present and active himself. The bishop of the see of Rome is not, in this profound sense, even a vicar of Peter; rather is he a successor in the see (*cathedra*) of Peter and Paul, who in the great tradition of the church (and in the liturgy) continue to preside over the see of Rome where they gave their final witness, and have no personal successors.

In a broader sense, all Christian ministers, and in the episcopal tradition, all bishops in particular, are vicars of Christ: not in the sense of taking his place in his absence, but in the sense of mediating his presence and action. This is a characteristically Catholic and sacramental view of the ministry: Christian ministers embody, crystallize, make visible and available, even guarantee, the continuing gift and service which Christ the Lord himself unceasingly exercises throughout his body, the church. In discussion with Protestants (if one may still use the term in decent ecumenical discourse) about ministry, I have often felt that in talking about 'priests' Catholics and Protestants, usually without realizing it, are operating with opposite and conflicting models. To a Protestant a 'priest' is someone wrongfully inserted between me and God 'on the way up'. He rightly reacts, 'I need no other mediator than Jesus Christ; any other mediator derogates from the once-for-all and universal mediation of Jesus Christ'. To a Catholic, a 'priest' is the human agent who mediates between Christ and me 'on the way down': he makes Christ really present to me by embodying ('incarnating') his continuing and pervasive service, self-gift, ministry in the Spirit; he makes it real, human, available.

But, of course, the human minister can never *perfectly* mediate the continuing presence and saving action of Christ ('on the way down'), his lordship, his priesthood, his prophetic role, the inspiration of his Spirit. Only Christ the Lord (the risen Christ is meant, not the mortal Jesus of the past) has power, has authority, is infallible, in any absolute sense. Embodied in the Christian ministry is not only the saving action of God, but also the great and varied inadequacies of the human servant; not only the Spirit, but the flesh. Once again, it is only in the theological climate of an absent Christ and of a human ministry operating in his place that one could get the phenomenon of 'triumphalism', in which the church

under its leaders was credited absolutely with such qualities as
unity, holiness, catholicity, the possession of truth, power over
men's lives. A theological climate, too, in which the eschatol-
ogy of the New Testament had been pushed out of this world
into the next and become the four last things: hence the
church, the bride of Christ, could here and now be thought of
as the kingdom of God on earth, as spotless and all-beautiful;
hence whatever had developed in the church had done so
under the guidance of the Spirit, was simply God's doing and
will, and was above criticism. Rather is it the case that the
church in all her life and ministries has imperfectly mediated
the saving presence and activity of her Lord; that tradition is
always under the judgment of God, which can best be
discerned by opening it prayerfully to the judgment of
scripture taken as a whole; that the church is a pilgrim church
led by the Spirit towards the kingdom of Christ, an *ecclesia
semper reformanda* as Vatican II recognized.

2. *Christ gives gifts of his Spirit to all in his body (and indeed
outside it).*

Baptism signifies that new human life is caught up into, or is
infused with, the life that the Lord lives in his body: is born
anew. Confirmation signifies that this Christ-life grows and
flowers into gifts, the gifts of the Spirit. Our human talents and
characteristics as they develop are not simply 'for' our earthly
journey; they are for the building up of the body of Christ and
for the patient building of his kingdom on earth. Our abilities
and talents have another dimension and another meaning than
the this-worldly or natural one: they are gifts of the Spirit
which Christ sends from the Father.

   One needs to stress again the primacy of Christ's presence
and action. He does not give all his gifts to each. But *he* gives
gifts to each. They are his even when given: as he embodies his
action in ours, his gifts remain his presence and action, never
wholly and in an exclusive sense becoming our own, at our
disposal. They never become simply the possession of anyone,
however eminent, as powers to be passed on to others or to be
withheld, according to good pleasure or due form. We simply
cannot talk of bishops 'having the power' (as a possessed
commodity) to make others bishops or priests, 'having' a

power which they can transmit or not according to accepted rules; or of priests 'having the power' to celebrate the eucharist. Only the Lord gives gifts and powers. *He* celebrates the eucharist in his body the church.

He gives gifts to *all* in his body, and they are primarily for the health of the body and not for the advantage of the individual, though the two interlock: not the place to go into it, but we grow by self-giving, not by perfecting our ego and being 'authentic'. So all in the church are under obligation to encourage, to profit by, to develop, to harmonize with, the gifts given to each for the building up of Christ's body and of the kingdom.

3. *At any point in history there is only one 'theological absolute' about patterns of ministry, only one categorical imperative: the church must so structure its ministries as best to fulfil the mission given it by Christ in the circumstances of here and of today.*

The church was not founded by the Jesus who lived and died and rose again to preserve itself or its past. It was founded to give God's free salvation to all in word and deed. It was founded to establish Christ's kingship in the world. It was founded to be the vehicle and manifestation of his self-gift, his lordship, his priesthood.

The statement also asserts a negative. The church is not hung about with precedents, with traditions that have hardened into absolutes. It does not from its founding and history have to structure its ministries one way rather than another. It is free. It is bound only to seek and implement the best means of fulfilling the purpose for which it is continually sent into the world. If only we could believe that! How many sterile, futile, even puerile, discussions would be undercut. But to free the church and to let this theology of ministry operate one has to clear a lot of ground.

A colleague of mine once announced to a meeting of church leaders, 'Bishops are not part of the good news'. He did not mean that they are bad news. He meant that ministerial structures are not part of the gospel to be preached (not of faith), but means of preaching it. They are an essential means only if here and now they are (part of) the best means. But even then they are not 'of faith'. They do not become 'of faith' even if always and everywhere hitherto (which would be hard to show) they have been part of the best means; even if always and everywhere hitherto God has guided the church into this means. They remain at the secondary level of Christian values and open to question.

Clearing the ground

1. One has to begin with the New Testament. Some bald statements will have to take the place of decades and libraries of biblical study.

The historical (pre-resurrection) Jesus did not envisage the church. The church was founded by the sending of the Spirit to proclaim the risen Jesus and to initiate faith in him. Nor did the risen Christ in any series of appearances issue instructions about the church's ministry. There is no sign that Jesus' disciples were aware of having any such instructions. And for the first Christians Jesus' resurrection heralded the end as imminent, it inaugurated the resurrection of all: it is unimaginable that they could be thinking of church organization.

Various patterns of ministry emerge in the two or three generations attested by the New Testament. What is salient is that *all* shared variously in kingdom-building-gifts.

Patterns of government or direction which emerge owe a lot to Jewish practice: not surprisingly. It is obvious that when Paul wrote to Corinth, no one was 'in charge' there: he looked after the community from a distance, expecting the end in his own lifetime. What would be the point of 'structures'?

The Twelve are shadowy: they are not the same as apostles; they are probably founders of the Jerusalem church. The point about the Twelve is that they are twelve (tribes of Israel): they *are* initially the church, the true Israel. At the last supper Jesus commissioned 'the church' (in embryo) to celebrate his memorial; he was not ordaining priests. (Indeed, the idea that Jesus ordained the apostles priests at the last supper did not appear in the church for several centuries.) Jesus instituted the eucharist, and therefore by implication a eucharistic ministry. But he did not ordain anyone to it at the last supper: he commissioned the whole church to celebrate it.

There is no evidence in the New Testament about who could or could not preside at the eucharist. It is unimaginable that the baptized Christian community, the body of Christ, should *not* be able to celebrate the eucharist.

Apostles are missionaries (the word means that), not 'bishops' in the sense of resident directors of a local community. Peter probably played the key role in founding the Jerusalem church: but he ceased to be a bishop and became an apostle, and James (not one of the Twelve) then headed that church. In a general way, Jesus' choice of special followers and the prominence he gave to Peter, set a pattern for future roles of responsibility; but there is no direct or linear descent between Jesus' actions and the pattern that later became universal.

Christ through the Spirit founded a-church-with-a-ministry; not a ministry commissioned to produce a church; nor a shapeless community which delegated its powers to an official ministry. But the phrase 'institution by Christ' can only be used of the later set pattern of bishops and priests in the broad sense that they developed in the church under the guidance of the Spirit, as it meditated on the precedents set by Jesus, in changing historical circumstances.

2. In considering the development of bishops and priests something must be said about words. 'Bishop' means 'overseer'. At first, bodies of 'overseers' in some local churches seem to be the same as bodies of 'presbyters' (elders) in others. The single-bishop model was firmly entrenched by the second century, but we do not know when it became universal (or started at Rome). In this model the presbyters became second-order elders. By the third century bishops are called 'priests' (*sacerdotes, hiereis*). Later the word 'presbyter' became corrupted in English to 'priest', with a change of meaning.

The development has both 'revelatory' causes (Jesus' precedents, interaction with the New Testament, guidance of the Spirit) and historical causes: the church is irreducibly in history; the Spirit operates through the flesh. So one is not denying the guidance of the Spirit by pointing out some of the salient historical factors.

(*a*) The emergence of an official ministry began a process of absorption. Clerical ministries soon absorbed lay ministries (clergy had some education). Episcopal ministry took over much responsibility from presbyters, even at one time for preaching. Papal ministry went some way towards absorbing episcopal responsibilities and therefore powers. Vatican II can be seen as reversing the trend and initiating a process of devolution at all levels.

(*b*) The growing awareness of the eucharist as sacrifice, and a certain switch of emphasis from gospel to eucharist, enabled the Jewish high-priesthood to act as a model in a way it could not do before, because Christ had brought an end to the Jewish priesthood by fulfilling it in himself. The eucharist requires a single president, not a group of presidents. The bishop from the third century is openly referred to as high-priest.

(*c*) The stratification of Roman society into *ordines*, with clearly defined political and social roles, certainly contributed to the 'orders' of clergy and to the emergence of a clerical class or caste within the church, with priests 'above' laity, clergy over against people. There was Old Testament precedent, but had not Jesus ended all that?

(*d*) The prevailing philosophy of the early centuries was neo-platonism, with its model of descending orders of beings. Some argue that this model assisted the stratification and introduced the idea of sacred power given by God to the clergy and descending through their ranks to the people.

3. It has been argued that the universal development of the bishop-priest pattern, and the fact of its continuing unchallenged for centuries, is a clear indication of the guidance of the Spirit and of the will of God for his church: hence, that the pattern becomes normative, even if it cannot be traced directly back to Jesus and did not exist in the first generations. But one has to be careful of this argument. One cannot but be struck by the element of historical conditioning in the ministry's development. And such conditioning is entirely proper, because the church is always both historical and the body of Christ: specific needs, specific cultural settings and assumptions, will give rise to particular patterns as the embodiment for that day and age of Christ's ministry in his church.

But this implies that in our day and age (and we are just as historically conditioned – there is no timeless or ideal model) other patterns may press for realization. To look at the matter from the side of God's action, one must similarly say that, if the Spirit guided the church into those patterns there and then, the same Spirit can guide into other patterns here and now. This is what the Reformers were saying in the sixteenth century. They wished to reform the ministry to make it truer to the gospel and the church's mission. They were naive in trying to reform by restoring the New Testament pattern, both because there can be no putting the clock of history back, and because there is no New Testament pattern. The naivety of the Catholic reply lay in asserting that the traditional pattern had been directly instituted by Jesus Christ.

Papacy, episcopacy and councils are always both the guidance of God and the product of history, which always includes 'the flesh' or sinful aspect of man's response to God. Their roles have continually changed in the past and will change in the future. What really matters in the ecumenical dialogue is not the theory of papacy or of episcopacy, but how they function in practice. The one imperative lying on the church is so to structure its ministry as to fulfil its mission.

4. The idea that 'holy power' (for the celebration of the eucharist and the forgiveness of sins) is vested in the clergy, and is transmitted by ordination, has lost favour in Catholic theology. There is no evidence of such an idea in New Testament times, and it is tied up with the emergence of a clerical caste, if not with neo-platonic patterns of thought. One must distinguish carefully between necessary church rules for the proper ordering of the church's life and worship, and what the baptized community is, and is able to do. (The Council of Trent was careful not to rule out Jerome's opinion that priests could ordain, and that reserving ordination to bishops was a matter of church rule.) God's action is mediated and assured by church ministry but not confined to 'the official channels': they do not take his place. The baptized community is Christ's and must be able to celebrate the eucharist.

Christian values

A great number of Christian values have been discovered in the process of ordering the church's ministries over many centuries, in different cultural settings, in different political and social circumstances. Different Christian traditions emphasize different values in the infinitely complex ways in which the inexhaustible riches of Christ's ministry and service are reflected in human response, response always situated in particular historical circumstances and conditioned by them. What must be realized is that statements of Christian value are second-order statements arising from human experience. They are not 'of faith'. They are in a sense negotiable, not absolute. They can be blended with and modified by the values that others have experienced. It is not good enough that in church-unity negotiations this or that should be declared a matter of 'principle' and then become a non-adaptable sticking-point. All such Christian values should be open to modification and development for the sake of greater Christian values, such as the visible unity in life and mission of the church.

In the course of discussion we have slid from using the word 'ministry' for all God's gifts to all his people to restricting it to the official or 'ordained' ministries of the church. A word of clarification is needed. In the New Testament all the gifts (*charismata*) of the Spirit to members of the church are services, ministries: not given just for the perfecting of the individual, but to be spent for the health of the body. As the church developed structures of responsibility, some gifts were incorporated into these structures and became 'office' without ceasing to be gifts. The Latin word *munus* hits off both aspects, gift and office. All the baptized are *christifideles* (those with faith in Christ) and have gifts. In the case of the ordained their gifts have been incorporated into the structures of responsibility: they have become office without ceasing to be gifts, and without their bearers ceasing to be *christifideles*. (Vatican II gets into some difficulties with the concept of 'the laity', who can only be defined by what they are not.) So office has to be distinguished from gift, but ordained ministry is both. And so (to save words) it happens that in discussing a theology of ministry one is mainly talking about ordained ministry, unless it is obvious from the context that the gifts, services, ministries of all are being considered.

All churches have exercised direction and 'oversight' through a combination of episcopal persons and of synods, in varying proportions. The churches which do not have bishops nevertheless have episcopal persons with wider responsibilities than other or more junior ministers, and one of their main duties is personal pastoral care of those other ministers. Traditional Reformed objections to episcopacy have been against prelacy rather than against episcopacy as such.

Episcopacy is closely associated with a eucharistic view of the church as communion (*koinonia*) and has served through centuries to maintain the unity of the church as a communion of communions. In the past Protestants have tended to assert that apostolic succession lies in the faithful continuance of the church in the apostolic faith, life and mission, but without producing any clear criteria for such continuance. Catholics, concentrating on the criteria, have tended to reduce apostolic succession to episcopal pedigree. Today these approaches have come together, and the bishop, incorporated into the world-wide college of bishops, is seen as the effective sign of apostolic succession.

Among bishops there are primates in any episcopal church, and the papacy is not an isolated office. The papacy has in fact served to preserve unity in a world-wide church, and to be an effective sign of the *catholica ecclesia*: the Anglican Roman-Catholic International Commission sees a role for a universal primacy as serving the unity of the church.

How the papacy best preserves unity in any particular age is a variable historical factor, a matter of careful discernment of the responsibility and how best to fulfil it in changing situations, not a matter of God-given constitutional rights and powers. The question is how the unitive power of Christ may best be mediated.

If uniformity and central control were the hallmarks of the counter-reformation, then different patterns are needed to serve that unity in diversity which was a keynote of Vatican II from the *Constitution on the Liturgy* onwards. There may be mileage in the idea that distinctions should be made between the Pope's roles as bishop of the local church of Rome, as patriarch of a wider area (the Latin Church? or just of Italy?), and as universal primate of widely differing regional churches needing their due measure of independent decision. It is understandable that Rome should be very cautious. Unity in uniformity was inherited, and diversity and independence of decision must be assimilated in small doses which will not disrupt the given unity. But it is difficult for 'the flesh' to distinguish such prudence from the mere retention of power.

Protestant witness to Christian values has been an emphasis on the gospel over against some mechanistic dangers of the sacramental system, a rejection of worldly panoply in the ministry, and a serious attempt to give scope to God's gifts to all his people. 'Ministry of (to) Word and Sacrament' is legitimate as an emphasis but false as a disjunction leading to devaluation of the sacraments: the celebration of every sacrament includes both verbal and other active proclamation of the gospel. Words are only one form of communication and do not exist in isolation from other forms.

The phrase 'priesthood of the faithful' has proved a confusing irrelevance: it is of biblical origin, designating the worship given to God by the people he has chosen as a whole; not designating functions of individuals, least of all cultic functions, which were reserved in Israel to one tribe. What is of importance is that God gives different gifts to each and all for the building of the church and kingdom.

Today's questions

Today some confusion reigns. Priests 'for ever according to the order of Melchisedech' are laicized. The canonical action implies a theology, and a non-theology: that there is no permanent 'character' (the Greek word for a stamped impression on wax etc.) stamped somewhere on the ordinand (the soul?) which cannot be effaced. It all stems from Augustine's metaphor of the 'character' of baptism, the brand-mark stamped on the baptized as on the emperor's soldier to mark him for time and eternity as belonging to the king: hence baptism is permanent; so, once done it cannot be repeated. Next the character spread from baptism to confirmation, which has never been wholly separate from baptism. Only in the thirteenth century did the idea develop that ordination, too, gives a character, impresses a permanent stamp, marking the priest for time and eternity as different (and being the reason why ordination cannot be repeated): this surely reflects the development of a caste system, even while it proclaims the 'holiness' of the priest and of what is entrusted to him. (In scripture, people and things are holy because they are brought by the holy God into a special relationship with him, into his service: holy people, holy land, holy vessels, holy (sacred) priests. So 'holy' orders are holy because God has chosen priests for his service; at the same time the word 'orders' reflects the human tendency and indeed need to create class distinctions, and to set apart establishment figures, investing them with status symbols such as holy clothes, whereas Peter said mass in his shirt sleeves, so to speak.

What comes through from all this as far as baptism and ordination are concerned are the ideas that they are permanent and that they are unrepeatable. There is no need to turn Augustine's metaphor into a peculiar metaphysics of substance and accident, in which a person's being is permanently qualified in baptism, confirmation, ordination (or marriage), by a mark or seal upon the soul. The irreversibility of history is surely sufficient. He or she *has* been baptized and confirmed into the Christian community, or ordained (appointed, commissioned) in it, and the fact cannot be undone, scrubbed out. She and he *have* been married, have committed themselves to each other for life. Because baptism, confirmation and marriage are what they are, they are not repeatable: you cannot enter the Christian community or marry the same spouse twice. So, in respect of the irreversibility of the past, these sacraments do not differ from other events of past history. But baptism, confirmation, marriage and ordination are not only past events for the community and for those in these states, but they are also commitments (by parents and community in the case of infant baptism). They are first God's commitment to us, and then our commitment in response to God and to each other; or God's permanent commitment to us being 'earthed' and taking historical form, being embodied, in special moments of our experience. That is why and how they are sacraments. Baptism-confirmation and marriage are by their nature commitments for life. It does not follow that ordination is, or that it has to be, on the side of the individual or of the community. It is not of the nature of ordaining to appoint someone to responsibilities for life, or of the nature of offering oneself and one's gifts for 'office' to do so for the rest of one's life. It is deeply important for the church that many individuals *should* commit themselves for life, but not necessary that all should do so; nor that the community should be wholly bound by such a commitment however well or ill it works out. This appears to be acknowledged in the fact that some who did commit themselves for life are 'laicized', absolved from that commitment in order to engage, let it be said, in other commitments, other ministries. A bishop who has resigned does not have to 'still be' a bishop in some urgent metaphysical sense, but should obviously be treated as one if he wishes or if the community wishes.

We really do get ourselves into some tangles. Many of us remember Archbishop Thomas Roberts with deep and lasting affection. I have written elsewhere: 'Whatever one may think about the contents of *Humanae Vitae*, its timing was fantastic: it appeared in the middle of the Lambeth Conference 1968! A packed church which went to listen to Archbishop Thomas Roberts at Farm Street the Sunday after were dashed to hear him say that he never spoke on controversial issues in that Jesuit church, as his views were not necessarily those of his fellow Jesuits, and so he would preach on the gospel of the day, the Transfiguration. However, they picked up again when he said that Peter's remark, "Let us make three tabernacles . . .", seemed to indicate that the first pope had momentarily lost his head. Roberts, an impish, saintly and attractive character, who learned of his appointment to the archbishopric of Bombay from *The Universe*, and who had 'crossed' Rome by forcing her hand on the transfer of the see of Bombiay to an Indian successor, was a lone Catholic episcopal voice on nuclear disarmament and contraception; a godsend to the Catholic middle class and an embarrassment to the establishment, who were hoist with a theory of the special charisma of truth possessed by bishops'.[3] The establishment could so easily have discounted him if they had been able to say, 'You aren't a bishop any more and so have no share in the magisterium.' So, according to one's point of view, one might be inclined to think that the sometimes asinine law can work for the kingdom of God.

[3]*The Testing of the Churches*, ed. Rupert Davies, Epworth Press 1982, p. 19.

We have got ourselves into a bit of a tangle in the Roman Catholic Church over the revival of the permanent diaconate. By some it is seen as a stepping-stone to married priests; others see it blocking that (for good or ill) and as anti-feminist. Some object to clericalizing perfectly good laymen (the point will be taken up below). Others see it as too rigid and archaic (and let us not mistake archaism for theology), falling far short of the flexibility the church needs, even if a small step in the right direction. Meanwhile other churches talk about 'the historic threefold ministry of bishop, priest and deacon' in reassuring rhetoric belied by the facts: there is only a verbal connection between the table-servers of Acts 6.1–6 and the famous chaplains to bishops (not to presbyters), like Lawrence, who emerged in the third century and passed away shortly afterwards; the 'office' then ceased to exist for the intervening centuries except as a liturgical role. Meanwhile there arose hundreds, possibly thousands (it is one of the things the Holy Spirit is said not to know) of congregations of nuns who actually *were* the deacons of the church and have been for centuries, as any bishop and any religious order engaged on overseas missionary work knows perfectly well. But of course to give them official recognition (status, forsooth) as 'deacons' would lead to enormous complications. Women in holy orders! The next thing would be that they would have to be treated as part of the sacred magisterium. . . .

We have, thank God, got ourselves, if not into a tangle, into an anomalous position about married priests. It is now possible for married clergy of other churches who become Roman Catholics to be considered for ordination as priests. When a young Catholic man comes to me and asks, 'I want to be a priest, but I want to be married: what do I do?' do I say, 'You leave the church, become e.g. a Methodist, get married, get ordained, and then come back again'? It is simply not conceivable that for very long two kinds of priests should be working side by side, those who may be married and those who may not. And of course our bishops who agreed to the latest move are not naive and know this very well. And of course the question is a deeply serious one, not only for existing priests who want to marry. Nearly everywhere in the church, but with burning urgency in some large areas, the need for married priests has repeatedly been voiced, as part of the general awareness that the set patterns of official ministry must variously be loosened up to enable the church to fulfil her mission. Before too long surely some bishop will break ranks on this issue, convinced that his single duty to the Lord and the Lord's people comes first. Hesitations about married priests are made more incomprehensible by the rich experience all around us of other churches (or does the Holy Spirit dwell in them, but not speak through their experience?). That experience does not deny, it reinforces, the values of celibacy. But no one is arguing that priests *have* to be married. And I hope one hardly needs to add that religious life (in religious orders) for men and women is another matter.

Surely common sense has a basic role in theology, and should only be ousted if and when it must?

Then there is confusion about the ordained and the lay. We hear of 'lay ministers of the eucharist' (i.e. of Holy Communion), both men and women. As they are appointed to this office, and as office as function and responsibility entails office as position and status, they are *ad hoc* not 'lay'. To say they are 'commissioned' not 'ordained' is to play with words. Similarly there is alarm if occasionally in the Free Churches there is a 'lay president' of the eucharist. If he or she is appointed for that occasion, by the community or in a recognized process by ordinary ministers, then for that occasion she or he is not 'lay'. Theory lags behind practice. In many parts of the world – basic communities are a good example – team ministries of men and women operate, 'clerical' and 'lay'. The distinction begins to be blurred. But what does it matter what we call them (they are too busy to be bothered by identity tags) as long as Christ serves his people through them? The valuable (though not hard and fast) distinction is between those appointed to a ministry (service) and those simply using God-given gifts on their own initiative. The latter will use their gifts well if they assist, rather than duplicate or disrupt, the more structured ministries of the community that exist already.

Thus, whether women should be priests becomes the wrong question because of its many assumptions. Both sides of the equation need loosening up: for 'priests' substitute a great variety of appointed ministries; and for 'women' in the abstract substitute a great variety of women in a great variety of social and historical settings. It is not a timeless question. No question about the church's ministries is. There is an increasing need to loosen up the pattern or structure of the church's ministries and to erode or even forget the distinction between clerical and lay. Men or women could be appointed full-time or part-time to any ministry; they could be appointed for a particular place or a particular task, and not with theoretically universal commissioning; they could be appointed for a limited term. Maybe it was hard to see this in the centuries in which Western thought understood everything in terms of its timeless nature or essence. Now it is shouting itself from the roof tops and from the Third World.

However, one pastoral need pulls in the opposite direction from others. While it would be desirable for the church to exercise maximum flexibility so as best to fulfil its mission *here* and *today* (and so not necessarily do 'there' what it does 'here'), yet over-rapid changes would leave many not knowing who or where they are. Identity crisis all round. People need recognizable symbols to establish their identity, and this is true of both the ordained and the lay. Inherited patterns of ordained ministry provide such symbols, and they make for stability and a sense of direction. However, they should not be allowed to be strait-jackets which hinder rather than foster the mediation of Christ's ministry in his church. We cannot start all over again with a *tabula rasa*. We must start where we are. We have traditions, but are not bound by them: rather, should we be instructed by them, as incorporating experienced values, and yet continually adapt them to meet present-day demands. It is a time of rapid change, so the pressure for adaptation is bound to be great. The faith-statement that the church must always so structure its ministry as best to fulfil its mission is an ideal, it is formal and abstract; its translation into practice will always be difficult; it is a divine imperative which we will never perfectly fulfil; it is a divine summons into the future, reminding us that the gospel always challenges the law; that the challenge to be fully Christian is the challenge to be fully human, in the image of the New Man, Christ. (It took God to be fully human, which is what the doctrine of the incarnation is about.)

Finally, authority is one of the most talked-about subjects in
the theology of ministry. But it is rarely talked about in terms
of responsibility. It might get us somewhere if we discussed it
solely in terms of responsibility, and not in terms of inherited
rights and powers.

Authority is always 'over' other people. It derives from
responsibility for others and from no other source, and it is
accountable. Conversely, anyone with responsibility for
others must have authority or appropriate power to carry out
that responsibility: you cannot be accountable if you lack the
necessary means of carrying out a responsibility.

But responsibilities are of very different kinds, and so
therefore are authorities. The authority of a parent, of a prime
minister, of an army officer, of the captain of a team, of a head
teacher, are not the same though they will be like each other at
some points. One always has to ask exactly what the person is
responsible *for*, and only by focussing that can one decide on
the appropriate ways of carrying out the responsibility, i.e. of
exercising the authority. A large part of the responsibility of
appointed ministers will certainly be to develop, encourage,
lead and facilitate the use of the gifts the Lord gives to others,
and assist them to be responsible Christians. To define the
authority of the Pope, for instance, we need to ask what
exactly he is responsible *for*, in the real world here and now
around him. There seems to be an emerging consensus that
precisely as Pope, rather than Western Patriarch or Bishop of
the see of Rome, God gives him responsibility for the unity of
the Roman Catholic Church and for bringing about its unity
with other churches. On this basis one is then able to consider
what are the appropriate ways of carrying out this responsibility, what sort of things he has the right to do and we have the
duty to respect.

We are all responsible *to* the Lord for the gifts he gives us,
and for our use of them in his service. So in their use we are all,
whether appointed or using our gifts on our own initiative,
responsible to him for the unity, harmony, orderliness,
effectiveness of the whole body. And therefore we are
normally also responsible to others in the community for these
factors. For the discharge of some responsibilities, however,
appointed ministers may be responsible only to the Lord. For

instance, if bishops are guardians of the faith and responsible for the preaching and teaching of the true gospel, though they exercise this responsiblity together with their fellow bishops, there may come points at which one bishop has to say, 'Here I stand'. Again, in some matters an episcopal person has the power or authority to make decisions affecting others. This does not mean that he 'has the power' or 'has the authority' like some possessed commodity: it means that others have given him the responsibility of deciding and will therefore respect his decisions. But he makes the decisions and in so doing is not merely the executive of a wider body.

The various meanings of the word 'power' seem already to have been catered for. That of God-given powers, possessed as commodities, has no place. A person chosen for responsibility is chosen because he is thought to have the powers (abilities, capacities, qualities) to fulfil the responsibility. He then must have power to carry out his responsibilities, i.e. others must respect and comply with his decisions. They must obey. But the obedience of Christians is not obedience to 'the system', or a grudging compliance with those who have the power to displace us if we disobey. It is the obedience of faith, the recognizing of Christ the Lord, encountered in and mediated by the ministers of his body the church.

3

INFALLIBILITY

What is the problem?

What is the problem to which 'infallibility' has been offered as an answer?

The problem can best be indicated by a brief historical sketch. For a Christian there was first Jesus. He taught, he preached the kingdom of God, he offered God's salvation to all, he demonstrated this salvation from evil by miracles. Even in the course of his ministry his own understanding of what was the role assigned to him by his Father, what it meant to be 'the Messiah' the anointed Son of God, developed. He came to see that it meant rejection, suffering and death. Whether he predicted his resurrection is very doubtful, because the predictions found on his lips in the gospels look very much as if they had been written in after the event: we cannot rely on them. In any case, he said nothing about what it might mean to his disciples to be a community believing their Lord had been raised to share the life of God. His followers certainly did believe, both that God had raised him from the dead to eternal life (God's life), and that Jesus now sent them the Spirit, the life-force of God. They were convinced that it was he who was sending them the Spirit, and that he was doing so to form them into a community commissioned to preach the salvation God offered to all through their risen Lord. They became the church. They expressed their faith in a great variety of ways: in once-off letters; in records of what Jesus had said and done, which were organized, cross-fertilized, arranged for teaching, related to the developing situations in which they found themselves, and thus variously and over a period of thirty to sixty years took shape as our present gospels. It took nearly four centuries for the whole body of writings which we call the New Testament to be universally accepted in the by then widespread church as the authentic record of the origins of Christianity and of what the first two or three generations of believers believed. Meanwhile the church had continued and had faced and thought and written about all kinds of questions which had never occurred to those whose witness is recorded in the New Testament. And that witness itself records a developing awareness. It is not a systematic treatment. It raises all kinds of questions about what Christians should believe. For example: who exactly was Jesus, and what was and is his relation to the God of Israel whom he called 'Father'? What effect on us does his life, death and resurrection have? Does it affect everyone, even those who lived before this time, even those who lived after his time but had never heard of him, or only those who had heard of and believed in him? In short, what is the message of the New Testament on these and other central questions? What is the gospel which Christians should believe and preach? Councils of the church were convened to answer such central questions – putting to the New Testament and later Christian witness questions these witnesses had either answered diversely or had never asked and so never answered explicitly. Councils reached answers and issued statements and creeds, rarely satisfying the convictions of all the leaders and thinkers who had taken part in them.

So the question arises at all times: is the church reliable in its teaching? If it is, what are the criteria? How are any of us to know if and when the church is reliable in its teaching? The problem or question is first about the church, not about any of its leaders whether bishops or theologians or both.

The actual word 'infallibility' can introduce a false start. The word is Latin and means that the church is so guided by God in its teaching that it does 'not fail' in the mission he entrusted to it. But the word 'infallible' in English has so many overtones that one has to spend time spelling out all the things it does *not* mean. It *does* mean 'reliable in teaching' or, as it is a negative word, 'safeguarded from error'. It does *not* mean: that Pope or Council is specially inspired or has a particular revelation; that what is said is the last or best word on the issue in question; or even that it is particularly important. In any case one is talking about realities or truths revealed by God, such that human wisdom could not attain them by its own expertise. So it does *not* mean that a church authority is able to pronounce definitively and with ultimate authority on any matters, but only on those revealed by God in the life, death and resurrection of Jesus Christ. An infallible pronouncement, if there is one, has to be about Jesus Christ.

Developing doctrine: from systematic to pastoral?

It may be hard for us to realize that a sense of history was a discovery of the nineteenth century. Pretty recent. Previously people tended to assume, in the church as elsewhere, that things had always been the way they found them to be: e.g. that Jesus equipped the church with a Pope and bishops before ascending to heaven. But we have briefly seen that the origins of these offices are much more complex.

All doctrines in the church have developed, notably the doctrine of the Trinity. The New Testament is itself evidence of the development of belief and teaching from the day Jesus met his first disciples-to-be until two or three generations of Christian believers had spread themselves somewhat around the Roman Empire. So it would be absurd to imagine that the doctrine of the church's reliability in teaching had not itself developed, and was not destined to develop further.

But this is a particularly tricky area, because it involves an obvious circularity. The church is trying to 'define', to formulate clearly and authoritatively, its own reliability in teaching. But you have already to accept its reliability, if you are going to accept its teaching on its reliability in teaching! In other words, it can only be a matter of faith, not of demonstration. It can only be a matter of articulating as clearly as possible what is and always has been the church's faith in, or reliance on, the guidance of God's Spirit, and how the Spirit exercises this guidance in the church's concrete experience and history. Faith is always in God.

The idea of the church's reliability in teaching was there from the earliest times. The church in Council and the Pope on his own had repeatedly taught the traditional truth and condemned errors, and the assumption obviously was that they were reliable in doing so. There was always the assumption that God protected the church from error in its authoritative teaching. At the Council of Trent this was asserted in so many words with regard to the interpretation of scripture. But it was Vatican I which for the first time expressly considered and pronounced on the criteria and the organs of reliability in teaching. It did so in a strangely truncated fashion, so that it is reasonable to expect that this 'first stab' at a formal doctrine of reliability would undergo further development and modification. For Vatican I set out to produce a constitution on *the church* and to pronounce on the church's reliability in teaching. The statement on *papal* infallibility is in a document entitled 'Dogmatic Constitution on the Church' (*Pastor Aeternus*), and the Pope is said to possess 'the infallibility with which the divine Redeemer wished his Church to be endowed. . . . ' But the Council never produced a constitution on the church. Internal political pressures secured that, after an introduction on 'The Institution and Foundation of the Church', attention was turned to the primacy and authority of the see of Rome. Then the Franco-Prussian War broke out (1870) and put an end to Vatican I. One can argue that the Council teaches that the Pope possesses *that* infallibility with which the divine redeemer willed his church to be endowed — but we were never told with *what* infallibility the Lord wished his church to be endowed.

The internal political pressures were strong and the mood of the Vatican over-confident in two ways in particular. In the late nineteenth century the papacy finally lost its political authority with the demise of the Papal States and their absorption into the new Italy. The Vatican reacted by strongly asserting its spiritual and doctrinal authority. Secondly, in the counter-reformation theology of that and the preceding centuries there was a prevailing confidence about the *philosophia perennis*, the timeless truth-language, reality-reflecting language, of the schools. In articulating Christian doctrine one could continually add clear-edged and precise bricks to clear-cut and solid foundations. Today we realize that this 'timeless' language was no more than the European cultural heritage from Greece and (to a slight extent) Rome. Today we know that all languages are historically and culturally conditioned, and that (for instance) disastrous misunderstanding ensues if you read Paul through Graeco-Roman spectacles. We know that the human mind continually, out of new experience, puts new questions to reality out of new perspectives and insights, and that it no longer makes sense to talk of 'the' truth. Pluralism of perspective and therefore of languages has come to stay.

The result of Vatican I's definition in our time, assisted by the rapid growth of communications, has been a growing centralization of government in the Catholic Church, and a 'creeping infallibility' in the popular mind with regard to papal pronouncements. Any and every papal utterance tends to be regarded as 'the teaching of the church', indeed as the voice of God settling the issue once and for all. And this, even when one papal utterance quietly overturns a previous papal utterance, as in the case of the primary and secondary ends of marriage as taught by *Humanae Vitae* (1968) and *Casti Conubii* (1930). The result has been to polarize other churches in opposition to Roman claims, and to prevent their adequately seeing and facing the problem that still remains on our hands: how reliable is the church in its teaching, and what are the criteria of reliability?

It is, after all, a very serious problem. If every element of Christian belief and teaching is always open to question, then we have no certainty of any kind about Christian teaching, no reliability. And in that case we have no identity ourselves, and no gospel to preach to the world. Is the only alternative that every central tenet of Christian faith can be permanently fixed with complete clarity (even if not with comprehensive treatment) once and for all? This latter view is simply refuted by facts of history. A notable example is the flat contradiction between the teaching of Vatican II and the teaching of Lateran IV (1215) on the possibility of salvation for those outside the church. Other 'infallibilities' have been tried and have failed. The infallibility of private guidance is not worth discussing, even though the claim to it is quite prevalent. Most consistently, perhaps, the infallibility of scripture has been advocated. All Christians would agree that Christian doctrine is founded on and permanently remains under the judgment of scripture. But, apart from many other objections to scripture being an infallible guide, it is obvious that all supposedly Christian beliefs have been based on scripture and that it is among this maze that we are seeking to find our way. The approach of the Eastern churches (explicitly rejected by Vatican I) is that the pronouncement of an ecumenical council is ultimately reliable ('infallible') when it receives the consent of the church. But how do we decide when a council is ecumenical, or know if and when the church has consented? The whole church has never consented to any conciliar pronouncement. From this one begins to see that the problem is one of self-definition and begins to look more like a pastoral than a systematic problem. 'We will regard as non-church those who do not accept this council's statement'. Or, to put it another way: the narrower you draw the boundaries, the clearer is your package of certainties and your message, the more secure you feel about your own identity, and the more Christian believers you exclude. The definitions of supposedly ecumenical councils up to Vatican I have excluded more and more Christians throughout history. Conversely, the wider your comprehensiveness, the more you will include of those who wish to call themselves Christians, and the less you will be certain about your message and your identity.

In discussing authority in teaching with Anglicans it is important for Catholics to realize that they regard comprehensiveness as a *virtue*, not an innate weakness arising from their historical origins which they are unable to overcome. The Lambeth Conference 1968 set it out in convincing terms: 'In the mind of an Anglican comprehensiveness is not compromise. Nor is it to bargain one truth for another. It is not a sophisticated word for syncretism. Rather it implies that the apprehension of truth is a growing thing: we only gradually succeed in "knowing the truth" ... there is a continuing search for the whole truth. . . . We tend to applaud the wisdom of the rabbi Gamaliel's dictum that if a thing is not of God it will not last very long (Acts 5.38–9).'[1] However, I think it is reasonable to point out something to Anglicans. The most

[1]Lambeth 1968, *Resolutions and Reports*, SPCK 1968, p. 140.

striking thing about the Lambeth Conference, which I had the
privilege of attending as an observer in 1968, was that all the
bishops spoke English. One particularly polished performance, both as to content and as to diction, was given by an
Indian Archbishop. When I asked what explained him, I was
told: 'Oh, Eton and Balliol.' Anglicanism, and other British
churches, already have a secure basis of identity in their
cultural origin and (usually) in their locality: they are held
together by a non-theological cultural glue. Certainly Catholic
missionaries rode into Asia, Africa and Latin America
equipped with Western education and Western theology,
which they tended to equate with culture and with theology
tout court. But those days are over, and the problem facing the
Catholic Church since the first constitution of Vatican II,
namely that on the liturgy, has been that of unity in diversity.
As by degrees it ceases to have any basis of identity across the
world apart from its belief and practices, it simply cannot
afford too much comprehensiveness. It would not serve the
cause of Christ or help other churches, if it lost the unity with
which it began and simply disintegrated.

A 'relative' infallibility?

The Final Report of ARCIC (*not* an infallible pronouncement) has an interesting pointer:

> Roman Catholic tradition has used the term infallibility to
> describe guaranteed freedom from fundamental error in
> judgment. We agree that this is a term applicable uncondi-
> tionally only to God, and that to use it of a human being,
> even in highly restricted circumstances, can produce many
> misunderstandings.[2]

The implication appears to be that both Roman and Anglican
members of the commission agree that the term can be applied
only 'conditionally' to church authority. What might be meant
by 'conditionally' is not made clear. It cannot be meant that
church authority is simply or absolutely infallible under
certain conditions, because that is the position of Vatican I

[2]ARCIC, *The Final Report*, Catholic Truth Society and SPCK 1982, p. 97.

explicitly rejected by the Anglican partners to the statement.

The thrust of my previous chapter on the theology of ministry was, first, that only statements about Christ's continuing presence and action in the church can be matters of faith and hence 'definable' in the technical sense. Then, that Christian ministries mediate, but cannot mediate perfectly, the ministry of Christ. Further, particular ways in which the ministry of Christ has been and is embodied among believing Christians throughout history are not themselves part of the gospel but means to living and proclaiming the gospel. And one of the logical problems of Vatican I was the attempt by Catholic bishops to turn the ways in which they seek to fulfil their responsibility as guardians of the faith into part of the faith to be guarded. If the idea could be accepted that synodal bodies and primatial persons in the church have, in certain circumstances, an imperfect or relative reliability in teaching, mediating the absolute infallibility of God, then it could perhaps be recognized that today the churches are at a point where they are able to see that they have a common pastoral problem on their hands, and shared tools and shared experience for tackling it together.

One result of accepting the theology here advocated is to recognize that we have not got and never will have the kind of certainties about or criteria of Christian truth that we would like to have. We must in the end rely solely on the guidance of the Holy Spirit, who alone can preserve the church from error and lead it in the whole area of truth, and whose guidance can never be wholly deployed or translated into constitutional procedures. And we are more likely to be guided by the Spirit if we are aware of our inadequacies and limitations and are attentively listening for his voice, than if we are complacent about our traditions and our structures; if we are more on our knees than on seats of judgment. But an acceptance of 'relative infallibility' does not absolve us from the responsibility of doing the best we can with the means available to us.

Of course, to say that 'reliability in teaching' has become a pastoral problem is not to suggest that pastoral questions can exist in isolation from doctrinal ones. But today the 'systematics' of this question have all been done exhaustively. The desks of Rome and of Geneva are littered with agreed statements, backed up by volumes of research, on scripture and tradition and teaching authority. The churches have for the first time in history reached the point where they can face the practical question: How in the circumstances of today can we best safeguard the gospel of Christ? They should face it together.

Postscript on morals

In my book, *Christian Truth*,[3] I raised some questions about the church's reliability in teaching on moral questions. There is a major point and a minor point.

The minor point is that Vatican I slipped 'and morals' into its definition of papal infallibility without having discussed the question. It did so relying on a mistranslation of the Council of Trent pardonable in the state of scholarship at the time. Trent spoke of the church's authority in interpreting scripture in matters of *fides* and *mores*. But at the time of Trent *mores* meant customary observances not morals; and *fides* was used broadly to cover Christian beliefs and values for living (as we might today say 'the faith'), and not narrowly for the area of Christian doctrine alone. There was no advertence to moral questions, as there was no dispute in this area at the time.

The major point is the following: Vatican I and II make it abundantly clear that the church can only claim to have an authoritative voice and special guidance of the Spirit in matters which are strictly of divine revelation, to the exclusion of matters in which man's ordinary powers of reasoning and enquiry are fully competent. Vatican II spelled out that 'the infallibility, with which the divine Redeemer wished to endow his Church in defining doctrine pertaining to faith or morals, is coextensive with the deposit of revelation which must be religiously guarded and loyally and courageously expounded' (*Lumen Gentium*, n. 25). There are, of course, areas like human conduct where both revelation and natural reasoning are relevant; but in those areas the church's message must be the gospel, must be about insights into the values of being human and living humanly which derive from faith in Jesus

[3]*Christian Truth*, Darton, Longman and Todd 1975, pp. 62–3.

Christ, and cannot be 'simply ethical'. Obviously, in a general sense there are Christian insights into human values, such as the primacy of love and the creative power of self-sacrifice. Obviously, too, the Spirit guides the church in a general sense in discussing human goodness; this was what Trent included in 'the faith'. But any assertion that the Catholic Church can claim divine guidance to 'know the answers' when there is question of bringing general insights to bear on particular and complex moral issues, or that it has nothing to learn from the views of others, even other Christians, is to say the least highly problematic.

4

OTHER CHURCHES, OTHER FAITHS

The grace of Christ

'There is only one universal Church of the faithful, outside which no one whatever will be saved.' This authoritative pronouncement of the Fourth Lateran Council (1215), reinforced in the next century by Boniface VIII's Bull *Unam Sanctam* ('outside which there is neither salvation nor remission of sins'), is perhaps the clearest example of a definition of a General Council which was, in any normal understanding of words, contradicted by a later General Council:

> Those also can attain to everlasting salvation who through no fault of their own do not know the gospel of Christ or His Church, yet sincerely seek God and, moved by grace, strive by their deeds to do His will as it is known to them through the dictates of conscience. Nor does divine Providence deny the help necessary for salvation to those who, without blame on their part, have not yet arrived at an explicit knowledge of God, but who strive to live a good life, thanks to His grace. Whatever goodness or truth is found among them is looked upon by the Church as a preparation for the gospel. She regards such qualities as given by Him who enlightens all men that they may finally have life.[1]

Yet at the same time this is a most interesting example of development in doctrine and of the cumulative nature of

---

[1]Vatican II, *Constitution on the Church*, n. 16.

Christian theology. The truth that was being so vigorously asserted and defended in earlier centuries was not the one which was being focussed and verbalized, but a deeper truth underlying it.

To put the matter at its simplest. From the outset Christians believed that salvation, eternal life, was available only through the grace or gift of God won by Jesus Christ's life, death and resurrection. This was the major premiss. In the course of proclaiming this belief a minor premiss was assumed: only those who believe in Christ receive that gift. The conclusion is inescapable: only believing Christians can be saved. Thus was set up perhaps the greatest 'crux' of all Christian theology, which was only solved in this century. But, alas, it has not been only a theoretical problem. Christian responsibility for persecution of the Jews, for the pogroms, for the holocaust, is horrendous: it was fuelled not only by the memory of the crucifixion but by the conviction that God had rejected his people. Crusaders, fired by zeal to rescue the holy places from 'infidel' hands, were ruthless with those whom God had destined to damnation. If one reads accounts of the siege of Malta by the Turks, the blood runs cold at the heroic savagery of Christian knights and Ottoman Turks, each burning with the same conviction, that they could do nothing greater for God's glory than to send as many as possible of the other side speedily down to hell. Then the enemies of God chiefly in focus became other Christians, century after century. And if the horrors of Northern Ireland are based not on religious differences but on social, political and tribal antagonisms, they have nonetheless been powerfully and barbarically charged with the hatred of Christians for each other. *Tantum religio potuit suadere malorum*. Lucretius condemned religious belief that could lead to human sacrifice. When will the human sacrifice end?

'No salvation without the grace of Christ, but only Christians have it.' The major premiss is unassailable. In our day some Christian thinkers have tried to solve the problems to which it gives rise by abandoning it: Jesus was a prophet from God and a messenger of salvation, but only one among many that God has raised up in history in different parts of the world; a word of God, but not the definitive Word. But problems in theology are not solved that way, namely by declaring that they do not exist: choice of one half of a paradox to the exclusion of the other is simple-minded and used in harsher times to be called heresy (the Greek *haeresis* meaning choice). From the outset it was central to Christian belief that Jesus was determinative of the salvation of all men: there is no other name in which men can be saved. If someone living in Tierra del Fuego in 2000 BC could possess eternal life and get to heaven without the gift of God through Jesus Christ, then Jesus' life and death and resurrection were not necessary for him; and if not necessary for him, then not for anyone. That destroys, not *a* Christian belief, but the core of Christian belief which is that Jesus Christ is not just a messenger from God but himself the definitive message: in Christ is life eternal for man and the meaning of life and history.

So it is the minor premiss that has to give way, namely that only Christians receive the gift of God through Christ (the grace of Christ). It was never very absolute. From the New Testament onwards there was recognition that the new covenant grew out of the old as its fulfilment, that Israel's history was the opening bars and first movement of God's plan of salvation for man. So throughout their history the Jews were unwittingly aspiring to Christ and could be seen as open to the salvation that comes from him. The issue was complicated by the need for baptism, but the notion of 'aspiring' (implicit faith in Christ) was stretched to cover catechumens who died before they were baptized, especially if they gave the witness of martyrdom. (And the church illogically celebrated the Feast of the Holy Innocents: oddly, not only because in the story they were killed willy-nilly in Herod's attempt to liquidate the rival king whose star had arisen in the east, but also because they were aged two years and under.) But this left vast numbers of the human race unaccounted for: first, all the non-Jewish peoples who had lived before Christ; then all the 'AD peoples' who had never heard the gospel. And one must remember, even before the discovery of America and Australia, how limited was geographical knowledge. Paul seemed to imagine that the gospel had been preached throughout the world in his own time, and everyone had had their chance. But what about infants who died in infancy, and did so in great numbers in the ancient world? They could not go to heaven if unbaptized; they could not go to hell because incapable of sin. So theologians invented limbo for them, a 'place' of natural happiness: it was not clear whether they were just souls (in which case natural happiness might be somewhat limited for infants) or were soul and body, unaccountably benefitting from the resurrection of the Lord. Theologians then fastened on limbo as the solution to the dilemma of a good and merciful God, while only Christians could be saved: the pagans were after all not to blame for their primitive religious and moral ideas; they were morally infants, deprived of the light rather than sinning against it. Counter-reformation theology happily consigned the vast majority of the human race to limbo thereby demonstrating the futility of the idea. God, it appeared, had not created man for himself, in his image and likeness, but only a miniscule proportion of men and women. The solution of one problem raised a larger one. Limbo faded quietly from the text-book and the pulpit.

There are two traditions or strands in the Old Testament, the inclusive and the exclusive. Israel sometimes understands herself as the people whom God's spontaneous love has chosen to be his own, to the exclusion of all others (and God's enemies are Israel's enemies). Sometimes Israel is proclaimed as chosen by God to be the light set on the hill (Sion) and shining abroad among the nations, the sign of God's love and care for all. The two strands continue in the New Testament, the inclusive prominent in Paul, the exclusive in John who in many ways deals in dichotomies of light and dark. In the long and sometimes tortuous argument in Romans 9–11, Paul is not thinking of the salvation of individuals (any more than he is in the 'predestination' passages of chapter 8) but wrestling with the puzzle of the Jewish rejection of Jesus. True, the first believers in Jesus were Jews, the holy remnant, the true Israel; but the fact remained that the people as a whole had rejected him, even after the resurrection. What can God's plan be? The Old Testament speaks on every page of God's love for Israel and his faithfulness to his promise of their salvation. That is God's plan, undeniably. And surely man cannot frustrate God's plan? God is faithful, as so often in past history, when man is not: his promise and covenant are irrevocable (Rom. 11.29). Ah, light dawns! God surely willed that Israel should refuse faith in Christ for a (short) time so that the gospel should be preached to the gentiles and that they should come to believe in Christ (this was precisely Paul's ministry). Then the Jews would be converted, and God would save all. 'For from him and through him and to him are all things. To him be glory for ever. Amen' (Rom. 11.25–36). Paul's answer to the problem is historically wrong, because the Jews did not come to believe in Christ; but it is theologically right: God's plan is to offer salvation to all.

It may seem extraordinary to us that it took so many centuries, so many convolutions of theological thinking, so much blood and hatred to which no New Testament writer would have given any sanction, to reach Vatican II. But eventually the hard core of systematic logic broke through. It is quite meaningless to say that Christ died for all, if his death has no effect on the vast majority of the human race; or to say that God wills all to be saved (the repeatedly quoted I Tim. 2.4), if practically none of them even has the chance of salvation and eternal life – a state of affairs that would also be morally offensive. Therefore the grace of Christ – not just some indefinable 'grace of God' but the self-gift of God mediated by Jesus Christ – must reach everyone. (Which is not to say that all are saved, but that all receive the possibility of salvation, the offer of eternal life, which they are free to accept and foster, or to reject.)

How this can be has been the subject of discussion among systematic theologians for many generations. It has been the life work of Karl Rahner to offer an answer to the question in terms of a rigidly philosophical understanding of human intellect and will, and it is to say the least somewhat irritating when his views are casually set aside by writers who do not seem to have grasped even the question at issue. For a long time in Western theology, under the influence of the prevailing scholastic system, 'grace' tended to be treated as a thing, a commodity, of which God had a store and which he dispensed at his choice. Actual graces were regarded as gifts of God, an unceasing multitude of little and somewhat arbitrary interventions, to adapt and transform nature, so that nature might be so moulded as to make it capable of sharing the life of God: the personal union of the being of God with 'the soul' was seen as the result or effect of actual graces, created graces; uncreated grace, the gift of God himself, as the effect of created grace (mouldings and modifications of human nature). In the nineteenth century the picture was upended by the work of Möhler and Scheeben in recovering the patristic perspectives: the gift of God's self was seen to be primary and causative (with a quasi-formal causality) and the transformation of nature was understood as the result. What is primary and fundamental is the personal, the establishing of a life-sharing personal relationship with man by God's gift of himself.

The 'grace of Christ', then, cannot be understood or imagined as some heavenly store of gifts, won by Jesus for mankind, and at God the Father's free disposal. The grace of Christ can only mean a personal relationship with God the Father mediated by Christ; or a personal relationship with Christ which establishes an involvement in the family life of God because Christ is eternal Son of the Father. But the question for theology *then* is: how can *that* be the case for those who lived before Christ, or for AD people who have never heard of him? *If* it is the case for them, for everyone in history, then it is constitutive of being human, constitutive of the human experience of life in this world, to have such a relationship with God. Indeed, it has been the aim of Rahner to set up a conceptual pattern to accommodate this basic truth about human beings, that a personal relationship with Christ, or at least the offer of one on God's part, is precisely what gives human beings the specifically spiritual qualities of experience which make them human and differentiate them from other forms of animal life. The grace of Christ is then gratuitous, not because it is given to some and not others (Augustine was hung up about this), but because through and through it springs from God's initiative and free gift of himself. One may or may not be entirely happy with Rahner's conceptual pattern – and no human conceptual system is going to grasp and deploy the mystery of God's self-gift to humanity without remainder – but at least he has focussed the problem correctly and has tried to solve it. The only meaningful way to criticize his solution is to produce a better one.

But, to step back a bit from the complexities of philosophical patterns of understanding human beings in their spirituality, the reader may have been left some way back wondering how it can make any sort of sense to talk of it being pervasive in, even constitutive of, human experience to have (the offer of) a personal relationship with Jesus Christ. It has, of course, to be the risen Lord and not simply the mortal Jesus about whom we are speaking. And, as I have argued elsewhere,[2] the object of Christian faith and the good news preached from the beginning always was and always has been Jesus of Nazareth who lived, died on the cross, was raised by the Father to share his life and who pours out that life (Spirit) on us. Never just the mortal Jesus in his teaching, works and death. And, to stop well short of philosophical anthropologies and to set up an overtly pictorial model to assist our understanding, we may well be able to imagine that the risen-ness of Jesus (his being gathered by the Father to share his life fully and give that life to us), being a reality outside time or 'above' time and not an event within human history like his life and death, is capable of having an effect on all time and all history.

But there are other models. An attractive one (favoured by Rahner) is sketched by Teilhard de Chardin. It involves recognizing that God did not have two plans, 'first' of creating nature and 'then' of giving to humanity a share in his own life. He only ever had one plan (as the Bible witnesses throughout), the kingdom of Christ, and his creation of the world was the first step to its fulfilment: the created world must be understood theologically as within the sphere of God's personal relation to humanity, and not as some substratum to it; nature is not a separate, bounded, 'order' intelligible in itself, but the material on which God works to transform it into his kingdom. (Hence the resistance of theologians to all 'complete explanations' of the human world by the natural or human sciences, severally or all together.) In this model (and if you change your model the interrelationship of all the constitutive elements changes) the end explains the beginning, the causality is final (purposive) rather than efficient: the force, the life-force, that ultimately explains why and how the world originated and how it develops, is the Spirit of the risen Lord, the Spirit sent from the Father through the Son to build the

[2]*Faith in Jesus Christ*, Darton, Longman and Todd 1980.

kingdom. In this model, 'incarnation' is seen not as an entry by God into human history from outside – an irruption – but as an eruption, the bursting through into definitive human form of the life-force and self-gift of God that is there at work from the beginning, continuous with the originating and continuing work of the Spirit, but also discontinuous and totally new. Those thinkers who do not like to put God 'outside' time, but see him as immanent in and involved by his own being in the creative and sustaining process, though in a transcendent way, will be able to elaborate the model along those lines.

Any new theological insights in one major area are likely to affect all others. The theology of redemption (or atonement, or whatever umbrella word one uses to cover all ideas and symbols for the meaning and efficacy of the saving work of Christ) has led in history not only to a great variety of 'explanations' but to not a few controversies and even antagonisms. That men are saved or justified by faith would seem to be obvious, if by 'saved' or 'justified' one means that they come to share in the eternal life of God, and if by 'faith' one means that they respond to God's initiating, creative and gratuitous offer of himself in a personal relationship, i.e. in love. But so far that says nothing about how the event of Jesus comes into it and affects us. 'Exemplarist' theories, those that in various ways bring out the truth that reflection on the life, works, teaching and death of Jesus changes our own lives and relates us to God personally in love and trust, have a long and honoured history in Christian thought. Their inadequacy lies in the obvious fact that they leave out in the cold those who have never heard of Jesus or never had Jesus adequately proclaimed to them, the vast majority of the human race. May it perhaps be that we should not try to penetrate the mystery of the risen Lord, the total filling and penetration of a man by the Spirit of God, when we are trying to understand in some sort of cause-effect terms how the event of Jesus affects all human life and history (experience); and look to the life and death of Jesus for our understanding of how acceptance of God's love for us works out in this life in real life terms? For the two are not separate or separable. It was the Jesus of history, the mortal Jesus, 'this man Jesus' as the author of Acts calls him, whom God raised from the dead to share his life and to share it with

us. The resurrection does not cancel out the cross in the sense
of obliterating a negative and putting a positive in its place, or
of correcting a deviation. It stands over all time and all human
experience (as in Salvador Dali's crucifixion picture 'St John of
the Cross'). *This* is what God involved himself in, this is what
God involved us in, in his self-gift to the void which drew out
of it Adam, man and his history – his history of love and hate,
hope and despair, tenderness and cruelty, ecstasy and suffering, annihilation and fulfilment.

Other religions

The effect on Christian attitudes to other faiths of recognizing
that the grace of Christ is at work in all, creating them as
persons and as human, is portentous. Negative attitudes are
not replaced by tolerance (a patronizing word) but by positive
attitudes, by respect, by reverence. Not only in religions, but
particularly in religions, is there witness to the grace of Christ.
Not only in Judaism, which has a special relationship to
Christianity, but in Islam, in Eastern religions, in African
religions, in all religions. Their ritual and cult is a way, their
way in their social and cultural and political situation, of
expressing their recognition of and response to the God and
Father of our Lord Jesus Christ who addresses them. Their
sacred books are 'inspired'. It is not a question of all or
nothing, any more than it is for the Jewish or Christian
scriptures. God's Spirit activates and works on people. They
express their awareness of his presence and action in them and
around them (their faith) in cultic ceremony and in various
styles of words: the words that are recognized and hailed by
others as witnessing their own view of God in life are hailed,
preserved, made classic, and become formative of future
experience and future expression of their faith. They become
'the writings'. They are witness both to the guidance and
impelling force of God's Spirit, and also to the limitations,
resistance, smallness, narrowness, blindness, of the flesh.
Neither in the Jewish and Christian scriptures nor in the classic
writings of other religions is it a case of all or nothing. It is a
matter of more and less.
   The relations between the religions and between the deno-

minations is one of the great issues of our time. Christians are aware that they have exported divisions to the developing countries of the world, the nations with a future rather than a past, not just their own divisions but east-west and north-south cultural divisions. But it is not just a matter of the relations of Christians to each other and to other faiths. It is also a question of the relation of Jews to Muslims, of Muslims to Muslims, all of which can lock neighbours in mortal combat and imperil the peace of the world. Love and hate are mingled. There is a dim awareness that those who believe in God (Yahweh, Allah the All-merciful, the Father of our Lord Jesus Christ) have something deeply in common over against those for whom 'God' has no bearing on real life. Is it something which more deeply unites them than all that appears to divide them, a vision and a faith? There is greater awareness that the forces that have so often led to hatred, war, cruelty, destruction, could become constructive forces of acceptance, of peace, of mutual support, even of love.

We are at the very rudimentary beginnings of the inter-faith dialogue. As with inter-Christian dialogue, it will have no value or constructive power amid the age-old forces of human tradition, if it is understood as accommodation, as compromise, as shaving off the edges of conviction and moving sideways in crablike fashion as in some bargaining process. It can only be fruitful and mutually fructifying as an exchange of sincerities; as a converging movement forwards towards a point of unity where each tradition will discover anew the fullest version and fulfilment of itself; a movement powered by learning from each other about ourselves; a search for truth in love. If we are all growing and developing – and in any one tradition we can see that happening – can we not grow, not by defining ourselves 'against the others', but by redefining ourselves in the light of the others?

At this rudimentary point in the interfaith dialogue, which may well be seen by later generations (who build on our efforts) to have set up its questions within too narrow parameters, there seem some insuperable obstacles. It is difficult to conduct dialogue with Hinduism because it is so syncretistic: its premiss that every religion is an equally valid way to God appears to deny the individuality of every religion

(except perhaps Hinduism) and to negate the Christian
conviction of the centrality of Christ; dialogue seems to be
between the 'intolerant superiority' of Christianity and the
'liberal toleration' of Hinduism; it appears to have no
'solution' but the absorption of Christianity by Hinduism.
Dialogue with Judaism and Islam is clearer because it is a
dialogue between definable convictions. The tension could be
creative. But, at this rudimentary point in the dialogue,
Christians are forced to ask: what would Judaism or Islam lose
of themselves by accepting Christianity? Christianity has
always seen itself as the break-through of Judaism (the religion
of Jesus) into its own newness and fulfilment: might it not be
the same with Islam? And where would that leave Judaism's
relation to Islam?

It may well be that at this early point in the dialogue the
fruitful common ground of exploration, at least between the
three great religions of Middle Eastern origin, is the doctrine of
the Spirit of God, the creative life-force of God, the power and
the wisdom, who operates in man's experience to open his eyes
to the recognition of the all-merciful Father creating us and
making us free and human by the gift of himself.

There is hope offered for the dialogue, not only between
religions but between all the main human stances in life, in the
attractive picture presented by some Fathers of the church:
Adam fell from the height at which God had placed him and
shattered in pieces across the world; Christ came, the new
Adam, to gather all the pieces and fashion them into one.

Where is the church?

And where in all this is the church?

Christians may at first feel threatened by the consequences
of this theology of the grace of Christ being offered to all and
being constitutive of all human experience and history. They
may be unnerved at the stripping away of some attitudes and
assumptions, and sense a loss of their identity at what is being
denied, before they discover the gain in what is being asserted.
Christians have to recognize that they are not the community
of grace, in the sense that they alone have or live in the grace of
Christ; they are not the community of believers set in black

and white contrast over against those who have no faith and need to be converted to faith. What then, in positive terms, is the church? What is its privilege?

The church is the community in which what God has done for all in Christ comes to full recognition and flower, and which is therefore a witness in the world both to who God is for humanity and to what humanity is, what it is to be fully human. It is not just a question of knowledge, of information, of knowing *about* God. The Christian is privileged to 'know' God, in the full biblical sense, to be personally aware of and attuned to him as he is, in a uniquely rich and full way; he is capable of a fuller faith, i.e. response to the God who gives himself, which opens up immeasurable possibilities of meaning in life. And the Christian is privileged to proclaim Christ, the way to truth and life, to the world, and so to invite others into a great expansion of their spirituality, humanness, immersion in life in its full sweep and richness.

In 'the old days' heroic missionaries gave their lives to working in distant lands and (to them) disease-ridden climates, to save the millions of benighted souls who were otherwise cascading into hell. What now can be the evangelizing or missionary motive, if it is not the basic question of salvation? The emphasis switches from the negative minimum of salvation to the fullness of Christ himself. The missionary can rejoice to welcome the Lord and respect the grace of Christ already present and at work in other peoples, other cultures, other faiths. At the same time it is principally for the love of the Lord that he or she can undertake the hardships and privations of missionary life: that the partly groping and undeveloped faith of peoples may come to know itself for what it is, and blossom into its maturity; that the Lord may be explicitly known and loved. It is strictly not the duty of the church to convert mankind to Christianity, but to proclaim the gospel in word and deed and to strive to build the kingdom. Faith in its fullness remains mysteriously God's gift and humanity's free response. The church remains a small minority of the human race: even if absolutely it may be growing in numbers, relatively to the growth of population, especially in China and India, it is becoming an even smaller minority. The church, it can be argued, cannot be judged by its effectiveness in making people Christians, but only by the clarity and purity of its witness, a leaven in the mass. At the same time one can hardly fail to be aware of the danger of rationalization in expounding such a theology: it sounds very like making the best of failure; and it may well avoid asking the question whether so far the church has really deserved to convert peoples massively to Christ. It may well be that a church which regarded itself as the one ark of salvation and despised other religions, and therefore other cultures, a church which imported divisions into indigenous cultures, was itself too immature to draw men to Christ, especially in age-old civilizations. It may well be that a church which is humble, which reflects the lineaments of the Servant, which seeks genuine dialogue without clearly seeing the outcome or knowing the answers in advance, a church which can receive as well as give, learn as well as teach, may yet prove far more suited to its missionary task.

But who and where, you may be asking, is this church of which we speak, if the humanity and the religions of all are already witness to the grace of Christ? The old adage seems to be turned on its head: not 'outside the church no salvation' but merely 'outside salvation no church'. Irenaeus wrote some often quoted words: 'For where the church is, there too is the Spirit of God.' No difficulty about that. But then he converted the proposition and added: 'and where the Spirit of God is, there is the church and every grace; but the Spirit is truth' (*Adv. Haer.* 3.24.1). So, wherever the Spirit is to be found in human experience, there is the church at least in germ. Which seems to suggest that all is church, to a greater or lesser extent of self-realization, except where God's grace, God's gift of himself, has been definitively rejected.

Well, exactly, that is precisely the problem of self definition for the church. Today's problem. Yesterday, and it was only yesterday, all non-Christians were without grace and went to hell (or limbo) – except perhaps the Jews; and Jerome had a soft spot for Plato and some other good pagans like the emperor Trajan, who surely must have had secret access to the Bible, i.e. to God's revelation. . . . Yesterday, only the true church had even the chance to go to heaven, and to listen to the preachers not many of them succeeded. ('It must, of course, be held as a matter of faith that outside the apostolic Roman

Church no one can be saved, that the Church is the one ark of salvation, and that whoever does not enter it will perish in the flood': Pius IX, 1854.) Protestants were black Protestants, or Rome was the scarlet woman.

We have grown up fast in my lifetime, or let us hope we have. The realization, the joyful dawning of awareness, that Christ is not far up in heaven so that the (true) church is in his place on earth, but that he is Lord of life and history and is everywhere in the kingdom of this world which is irrevocably his own – this really does relativize the differences between Christians. In a very broad sense one must say that the church is the *body* of Christ. If all is church, nothing is church. So by 'church' one must mean those who openly recognize and confess Christ; those in and among whom the Lordship of Christ is explicitly confessed and so embodied in history. For the Lord is after all the man-in-history, Jesus of Nazareth, now seated at the right hand of the Father to pour out his Spirit in the world: he is incarnate, embodied in and visibly part of history. One could take the World Council of Churches' basis (1961) and say that they are the church who 'confess the Lord Jesus Christ as God and Saviour according to the scriptures'.

The joyful recognition that the grace of Christ is available to all men provides a wholly new context within which the various Christian churches consider their differences and seek to heal their divisions. Just as there now appears to be a certain continuity and not a total break between Christianity and non-Christian religions, so there is discussion between Christian traditions as to what among these traditions might constitute the fullness of the church, today or in the future. In place of the old exclusivist attitudes – we are the true church, the right version of the church, the way God meant the church to be – there is a growing realization that Christian tradition is and always has been pluriform, that none of the traditions can by itself claim to be or to have the fullness of the church, and that for the future a new sort of unity in diversity might constitute a new fullness of the church, a new catholicity, a fullness and a unity that have not previously existed.

Such a church might well be more effective in proclaiming the gospel of Christ among peoples with whom it has meanwhile established relationships of growing understanding and trust.

5

INTERCHURCH MARRIAGE

An area in which there has been considerable development since Vatican II in theological reflection and pastoral practice is that of mixed marriages. There was always a difference in law between the dispensation a Catholic required to marry a baptized Christian of another communion (misnamed *a mixta religione*, and needed only for the lawfulness of the marriage), and the dispensation he or she required to marry a non-Christian (*a disparitate cultus*, and required for validity). But this was a technical difference, and both classes were mentally lumped together as 'non-Catholics': a committed Protestant could thus be classed with and treated the same as an agnostic. Since the Decree on Ecumenism, it has been increasingly recognized that Catholics are in imperfect or partial communion with other Christians in the body of Christ,[1] and specially linked to them by the bond of baptism;[2] and this has progressively affected the handling of mixed marriages of Catholics with other Christians. A further influence has been the *Declaration on Religious Freedom*, a document referred to by the Pope in his apostolic letter, *Matrimonia Mixta*, of March 1970, which governed practice until the new code of Canon Law.[3] At Vatican II, the church became more aware of the danger of her violating the rights of conscience of the non-Catholic party in a mixed marriage.

[1] *Unitatis Redintegratio*, 3.
[2] Ibid., 22.
[3] The English text of *Matrimonia Mixta* is published, together with the official Directory of the English and Welsh Bishops, by The Catholic Truth Society as *Mixed Marriages*.

A statement such as the following, even if made primarily to assert the rights of the individual vis-a-vis the civil power, is broad and deep enough to include interchurch relations: 'This [religious] freedom means that all men are to be immune from coercion on the part of individuals or of social groups and of any human power, in such wise that in matters religious no one is to be forced to act in a manner contrary to his own beliefs'.[4]

In Britain it is often estimated that about seventy per cent of Catholic marriages are mixed, and of these the vast majority, perhaps as many as ninety per cent, are between Catholics who must have some measure of commitment (or they would not approach the priest at all) and those of no religion. From these facts two things follow. The first is a very deep and justifiable concern on the part of bishops and priests that Catholic faith and life should be perpetuated and strengthened in the Catholic party, and should be imparted to the children. But it also often results that the true 'interchurch' marriage, namely one between a committed Catholic and a committed Christian of another communion, is overlooked and is classed with, and handled like, a 'merely mixed' marriage. It is with interchurch marriages that this chapter is chiefly concerned, in the belief that they need and deserve special and careful attention. First, because of the truly conscientious and Christian conviction of the non-Catholic. Secondly because of the particular pastoral needs of both. Thirdly because, though such marriages may be comparatively few in number, they are qualitatively of great importance in the ecumenical scene. The way they are handled or pastorally cared for can have considerable effects, for good or for ill, on the relations between the churches themselves. In the more local scene, the interchurch couple, who are learning to live a united Christian life, can be a considerable ecumenical force and focus: they are bound to each other by the sacramental bond of marriage over and above that of baptism; they have a more deep Christian commitment to each other than their churches have; they are more fully in communion with each other than their churches; they have a personal experience of Christian unity which they can communicate to others, and they can even be seen as an eschatological sign of

[4] *Declaration on Religious Freedom (Dignitatis Humanae)*, 2.

the unity we seek.[5] Finally, they can have an influence on the 'merely mixed' marriages that are all around them: the simplest solution to religious differences in a marriage is not to have any religion at all, and it is a solution eventually followed by a large number of mixed marriages; the interchurch couple can give a positive lead to others. (At the centre of interchurch marriages is the increasing number of Anglican priests with Catholic wives. I know personally ten such couples in England, and one in Dublin; and there are no doubt many more.)

Permission to marry

Before the new Code of Canon Law the fact that the intended partner of the Catholic was a baptized non-Catholic constituted a canonical impediment (the inappropriately named *mixta religio*), from which the Catholic needed a dispensation before the marriage could go ahead. If the marriage had gone ahead without any dispensation, it would have been valid; but in practice no Catholic priest would have celebrated it. The new Code has abolished the impediment and the need of a dispensation from it. But it still requires permission of the 'competent authority' (the bishop or those to whom he has delegated the power to give such permission). So it comes to the same thing.

The arguments for retaining the need to get permission are as follows. The church naturally wishes Catholics to marry Catholics, both because of the need of unity at this central point of life, and to ensure that the home life of the faithful will nourish their Catholic faith and that of their children. Even forty years ago some bishops made difficulties about granting a dispensation, in order to discourage mixed marriages as far as possible. Old Canon Law (1060) even said that 'the church most severely prohibits' such marriages; but the canons on this

[5]Cf. *Matrimonia Mixta*, para. b. In their Directory the French bishops express their joy that some mixed marriages 'through often painful tensions, light up and help forward the ecumenical journey of the churches themselves'. See *One in Christ*, VII, 1971, p. 222. Similarly the Belgian bishops (ibid., p. 223): 'In the little church of their family they can also be a prefiguration of the Christian unity which is yet to come'.

matter were replaced by the Pope's letter, *Matrimonia Mixta*, which spoke more leniently and understandingly, and required only a *iusta causa* (i.e. a good reason), in place of the 'grave' reason of the Code, for the granting of the dispensation. This is reflected in the new Code as a *iusta et rationabilis causa*. In practice, in Britain, the permission is given for the asking, once the relevant promises have been made. It might be argued that a law which is always dispensed with should be abolished, as it becomes meaningless and brings law in general into disrepute. But the reality of the matter lies, not in the permission, but in the annexed promises which are the condition of the permission being granted. And the argument for keeping these is that they enable priests to face possibly euphoric couples with their profound Christian obligations, and to help them to give serious consideration, in good time, to the problems that are inherent in any mixed marriage. They are also an occasion of bringing out into the open, for the sake of both partners, the Catholic conviction that the Catholic Church is the fullest visible and sacramental expression in history of all that Christ wished his church to be. (As is well known, the Council avoided the expression 'the true church', and spoke of the church of Christ 'subsisting' in the Roman Catholic Church.) In view of the facts and figures about mixed marriages, already outlined, this is obviously a very serious consideration indeed, not only for the particular couple, but for the Catholic Church in this country.

There are, however, arguments against retaining the permission and the attached promises. (The latter would have to go, if the former were removed, for otherwise the requirement of formal promises would itself act as an impediment: indeed, in practice, it is they that now constitute the actual support for Catholic teaching and the hurdle to be cleared.) The chief argument is that the need to ask permission causes considerable offence to other churches: a Catholic needs permission to marry 'one of them'. It is this kind of barrier that is seen (rightly or wrongly) as evidence of lack of full sincerity on the part of the Catholic Church in the ecumenical movement. Its removal would do a lot to improve relations with other churches; it would be seen as concrete evidence that the Catholic Church really accepts the baptism of other churches, really recognizes the genuineness of their Christian life, and is serious about brotherly relationships with them and desire for unity. Hence the Catholic Church is faced with a choice between what seems good for the care of her own faithful, and what is increasingly demanded by the growing union of the churches and the progressive relationships that this involves. It would still be possible and desirable for priests to instruct Catholics and their proposed partners carefully about Catholic conviction and the challenges of a mixed marriage, if there were no permission and no promises. Other churches find the Catholic Church too prone to hedge conscience with law, and think that this keeps the faithful in a state of religious immaturity. And they (and Catholics too) find it distasteful to involve the sacred and personal occasion of marriage with more legal requirements than are already necessary. The contrary opinion would be that a certain measure of discipline is healthy as a way of proclaiming one's faith and insisting on the importance of certain obligations. But the chief argument against retaining the rule of having to ask permission to marry a Christian of another communion is that, however much explaining one does in a coldly rational way – theological, canonical, even psychological – the fact remains that one church is laying down a condition and the other is not, and the couple very strongly resent one church introducing this imbalance into the deeply personal occasion and sacrament of union.

Some have argued that people have a natural right to marry whom they wish, and so question the right of the Catholic Church to introduce this condition.

The answer from the Catholic side is that the church does not (and of course cannot) prevent Catholics from marrying non-Catholics in the 'natural sense' of contracting a civil marriage. But it regards all Christians as raised by baptism to the visible order of grace, so that a further dimension is given by God's grace to their pledges of marriage, as to their whole lives. They *are* Christians (whose marriage has a meaning in and for their Christian community) and cannot cease to be so for the purpose of marriage; so in the eyes of the church their marriage is either a marriage within the Christian community, and an essential part of that community's life and self-perpetuation, or it is no marriage at all. Hence it is the Christian community's need and right to determine what shall be regarded as a Christian marriage. The impediment in question is an expression of the conviction that the Catholic Church is the church as Christ intended it to be, and is therefore an expression of her ecclesiology: that is, of her self-awareness as a Christian community.

The promise about the children

The new Code of Canon Law has the following canons about mixed marriages:

> *Can. 1124* Without the express permission of the competent authority, marriage is prohibited between two baptized persons, one of whom was baptized in the Catholic Church or received into it after baptism and has not defected from it by a formal act, the other of whom belongs to a church or ecclesial community not in full communion with the Catholic Church.

> *Can. 1125* The local Ordinary can grant this permission if there is a just and reasonable cause. He is not to grant it unless the following conditions are fulfilled:
> 1. The Catholic party is to declare that he or she is prepared to remove dangers of defecting from the faith, and is to make a sincere promise to do all in his or her power in order that all the children be baptized and brought up in the Catholic Church;
> 2. The other party is to be informed in good time of these promises to be made by the Catholic party, so that it is certain that he or she is truly aware of the promise and of the obligation of the Catholic party;
> 3. Both parties are to be instructed about the purposes and essential properties of marriage, which are not to be excluded by either contractant.

> *Can. 1126* It is for the Episcopal Conference to prescribe the manner in which these declarations and promises, which are always required, are to be made, and to determine how they are to be established in the external forum, and how the

non-Catholic party is to be informed of them.

Since the papal statement *Matrimonia Mixta* (1970) the non-Catholic party has not been required to make any promise: he or she is simply to be informed of the Catholic's undertakings, so as to be fully aware of the latter's position. The law does not require any reaction from them at all.

The Catholic's declaration about preserving his or her own faith has been found acceptable by all. It is the promise about the children which has caused the difficulties and needs careful discussion.

In Catholic conviction the church divinely instituted by God the Father through Jesus Christ 'subsists in' the Roman Catholic Church, is fully realized in that church and in no other. So for Catholics their church is not just one 'denomination' among others; it is central to God's plan for his church, it stands for the single *ecclesia catholica* across the world united by communion with the see of Rome. It follows that Catholics believe they have an obligation to bring up their children as Catholics, not simply as Christians in some Christian denomination.

It does not follow from Catholic conviction that, before mixed marriages Catholics should have to make a formal statement of their conviction in the form of a promise. This is a matter of positive ecclesiastical law which the church could abolish, or can dispense from; whereas it cannot abolish or dispense from an obligation in conscience arising from Catholic faith. Hence in requiring the promise about the children, the church is not imposing any additional obligation in conscience on Catholics, any more than in the case of the declaration about keeping the faith: it is simply requiring them to state in the form of a promise the obligation they already have.

A non-Catholic cannot be expected to accept that the Catholic Church is 'of divine law', or divine institution, in a way that overrides the claim of his or her own church to divine institution;[6] and the parent may very well have a firm contrary

[6]'The Anglican would acknowledge a divine law for Christians to offer a Christian upbringing to their children, but would question whether any narrower definition than this could be said to have "divine" sanction.' (Third Report of the Anglican/Roman Catholic Commission on Marriage, n. 12; cf. *One in Christ*, IX, 1973, p. 202.)

conviction that it is according to the will of Christ that the children be brought up in his or her own church. It has often not seriously occurred to, or been faced by, Catholics that other Christians may have equally deep counter-convictions of their own. The change in Catholic rules for mixed marriages is a recognition of the rights of conscience of the other party. The Declaration on Religious Freedom shows a consistency in terminology when it says: 'On his part man perceives and acknowledges the imperatives of the divine law through the mediation of his conscience'.[7] The conscience of the non-Catholic is the vehicle of divine law. The same Declaration later states: 'Since the family is a society in its own original right, it has the right freely to live its own domestic life under the guidance of parents. Parents, moreover, have the right to determine, in accordance with their own religious beliefs, the kind of religious education that their children are to receive'.[8] As the rest of the paragraph shows, these statements are made in the context of the parents' rights over against the civil power, but they obviously have their application to parents who acknowledge the authority of different churches and different theological traditions. They are reflected in the assertion of *Matrimonia Mixta*: 'The problem of the children's education is a particularly difficult one, in view of the fact that both husband and wife are bound by that responsibility and may by no means ignore it or any of the obligations connected with it'.[9]

The fact that the Catholic is required to state or acknowledge his or her conviction in the form of a promise, as we have seen, does not in any way add to the obligation in conscience which already exists: it merely states it. Stating it does not put any undue pressure on the conscience of the other party: it merely clarifies the existing position. Thus it in no way pre-empts the decision that will have to be made about the children.

It proves in practice extremely difficult for either Catholics or their non-Catholic partners to grasp these facts. Reasonably or unreasonably, both parties may feel a resentment about the

[7] *Dignitatis Humanae*, 3.
[8] Ibid., 5.
[9] Loc. cit., para j.

promise which it is difficult to banish. They continue to regard it as an extreme form of pressure on the conscience of the non-Catholic. One even hears such phrases as 'signing away the children', and of course the promise does nothing of the kind.

Hence it needs to be clearly restated, because it is not always understood on either side, that the Catholic does not promise that the children will in fact be baptized and brought up as Catholics: such a promise would indeed exert undue pressure on the conscience of the other. The promise is to do what can be done to bring this about. And that is what the individual's Catholic conviction already means, for it cannot be a sincere conviction unless he or she intends to do what can be done about it. What in fact this means in reality depends, not simply on the other, but on the way the relationship between the two partners develops.

The Anglican/Roman-Catholic commission on marriage rightly states: 'A pastoral purpose may require expression in juridical language and process: to legislators and administrators of the law this pastoral end should always be seen to be primary'.[10] It seems necessary in the matter of this promise to distinguish pastoral from legal concerns. In order to secure the permission to marry, the legal requirement is simply that the Catholic should make the promises and the other party be informed. No reaction is required from the latter, and their attitude to the children's religious upbringing does not need to be known. But, of course, pastorally it is quite inadequate for the priest concerned simply to 'polish off' legal formalities without helping the couple to face together, and to understand as fully as they can in advance, both the special challenges and the special opportunities which an interchurch marriage presents. In the course of such necessary discussion the priest can hardly fail to discover the non-Catholic's attitude to some extent. He may find that he or she has little or no Christian conviction, and so feel pretty sure that the children are to be brought up as Catholics. But he should not rejoice at the non-Catholic's lack of conviction on the ground that it presents 'no difficulties': the Catholic will get little or no help and support from marriage either for personal faith or for the children's

---

[10]Third Report, no. 4, *One in Christ*, IX, p. 199.

upbringing; it will not be a truly Christian family, with both parents taking a part in its religious life. The priest should not exclude the hope that being married to a good Catholic may make a poor Anglican (say) into a good Anglican; absence of Christian commitment is by no means a guarantee against religious squabbles, and commitment removes a main barrier to marital breakdown. The priest may, on the other hand, find that the non-Catholic cannot entertain the idea of his or her children being Catholics; or he may find that the non-Catholic is by far the more committed to his or her church of the two. Should he, in either of these situations, regard the conviction of the non-Catholic as a reason for not recommending the permission to marry even though it is not a legal requirement for that permission that the non-Catholic's attitude should even be known? And should the bishop regard the attitude of the non-Catholic as a reason for refusing the dispensation?

Before any answer to these questions is considered, one further matter of importance needs to be taken into account. It is not legally required for the granting of the dispensation that the couple should first reach a decision about the Christian upbringing of their children. Is it pastorally wise to bring them at this point to such a decision? Many priests seem to try to do this, and they may even think it (pastorally) necessary to do so. Nowhere does *Matrimonia Mixta* or The Code say so. They may even still think that permission to marry can only be granted if the non-Catholic is somehow 'talked round', and there is a moral certainty that the children will be brought up as Catholics. There is no suggestion of this in *Matrimonia Mixta*. The question of such moral certainty came into the arrangements prevailing between the papal Instruction of March 1966 and the Apostolic Letter of 1970: with such certainty the bishop could grant the dispensation, without it he had to apply to Rome. But it is part of the advance made by *Matrimonia Mixta* that it did not require such moral certainty for the bishop to grant the dispensation: he may now do what Rome repeatedly did in the intervening years, namely grant permission, as long as the Catholic has made the promises, even when it is morally certain that the children will be brought up as non-Catholics. So, it is not for *this* reason necessary that the couple should reach a decision about the children before they are married, or before they are given a dispensation to marry. The directories of the Swiss, Belgian, French and Canadian hierarchies show that they expect the decision to be one that will emerge in the course of the marrage.[11] So does the second report of the Anglican/Roman-Catholic commission on marriage: 'We acknowledge that as the spouses after their marriage "experience the meaning of their oneness and attain to it with growing perfection day by day" (*Gaudium et Spes*) they must be encouraged to come to a common mind in deciding factors relative to their conjugal and family life'.[12] There are strong arguments for this. At the pre-marital stage the couple have only begun to know each other and to learn about the other's church and religious convictions. They should be encouraged through joint prayer and worship, not only to deepen their understanding of each other's Christianity and their experience of a basically common faith, but to strive to reach a joint decision about the children which is truly acceptable to both and can therefore be carried out in full partnership. A hoped-for convergence of this kind takes time. Marriage is a uniting bond, a sacrament of union: the experience of marriage itself must be allowed to contribute to the formation of a joint decision.

Hence, to return to the question laid aside, it would seem to follow that the pastoral desirability of granting permission cannot be decided simply on what appear to be the attitudes of the partners at the pre-marital stage. Both may need to change. The Catholic may be weak in commitment and may be made a better Catholic by a committed Christian partner; or he or she may be over-rigid and exclusive, perhaps from upbringing and social pressures, and need to learn respect for other Christians through marriage. If the non-Catholic is hostile to Catholicism, the reverse is true: the lived faith of the Catholic partner must be trusted to show its worth and to bring the other partner progressively to respect it. One cannot exclude the possibility of cases (surely a very exceptional minority) in which the attitudes of the couple seem so implacably irreconcilable (and it is a question of the couple, and not simply of

[11]See *One in Christ*, VII, 1971, pp. 230–233; VIII, 1972, p. 425.
[12]Quoted in the Commission's third report, *One in Christ*, IX, 1973, p. 201.

the non-Catholic), that the pastor becomes quite convinced that the marriage would not work: this would then be the pastoral reason for witholding the dispensation, at any rate in the first instance, and persuading them, if possible, to give up their intention of marrying.

Some episcopal directories explicitly recognize that the couple may eventually and responsibly decide to bring up the children as members of a non-Catholic communion: in doing so they respect both the conscience of the non-Catholic, and the fact that responsibility for the decision truly rests with the couple, cannot be made for them, and needs for the sake of the marriage (and so of the children) to be a joint decision which both can approve and implement. The directory of the German bishops explains in some detail that, in that case, the Catholic is still bound to play an active part in the Christian upbringing of the children, and to lead them to a knowledge and understanding of Catholicism. Later in this chapter we will consider more fully the question to what extent the decision to bring up the children in one church is exclusive or inclusive of bringing them up in the other.

The Catholic promises to do what he or she can to ensure the Catholic baptism and upbringing of the children. *Matrimonia Mixta* uses two different phrases in this connection. In the introductory section it says: 'The Catholic partner is obliged, as far as possible, to see to it that. . . . '[13] In Norm 4 it says: ' . . . promise to do all in his power. . . . '[14] This stronger phrase causes difficulties, sometimes to both parties. It could be understood as a promise to exert pressure by any available means, but is obviously not meant in this sense: one could fairly gloss it by the earlier and gentler phrase. Nevertheless, it contributes to the pervasive impression that the whole demand for a promise on the Catholic side exerts undue moral pressure on the non-Catholic, and introduces an unnecessary dividing factor between the couple. Hence it needs explanation. The Anglican/Roman-Catholic commission on marriage reports: 'This English phrase might be and often is adduced to justify

[13]Pars catholica obligatione tenetur . . . quantum fieri potest, curandi ut . . .

[14]Pars catholica . . . promissionem . . . se omnia pro viribus facturam esse ut . . .

the Roman Catholic party acting in a way which disregards the equal rights in conscience of the non-Roman Catholic party, and even to justify the Roman Catholic adopting an attitude or pursuing his purpose in ways which might endanger the marriage. It is recognized that responsible Roman Catholic commentators on the letter (including many episcopal conferences) do not put this interpretation on the Latin phrase, but rather confirm our Windsor statement quoted above – viz. 'The duty to educate children in the Roman Catholic faith is circumscribed by other duties such as that of preserving the unity of the family'.[15] The directory of the Swiss bishops explains as follows: 'The religious education of the children is a duty shared by both partners. That is why the Catholic partner alone cannot commit himself to baptize and educate his children effectively in the Catholic faith. He must, however, desire to work for the Catholic baptism and education of his children so far as that is possible in the concrete circumstances of his marriage. To do what is possible in the concrete circumstances means: in sincere dialogue and in respect for the reasons and religious convictions of the partner, to make a decision which both can approve'. Similarly the Canadian bishops: 'To do one's utmost in the particular circumstances of this marriage means that the parties should arrive at a decision agreeable to both, after sincere discussions which take place with due respect for the religious conviction of the partner'.[16]

Finally, there is no doubt that having to *sign* a promise causes a further difficulty, sometimes to both parties. The friendly and pastoral discussion of priest and couple becomes awkward and embarrassing at this point. It is no good simply making the rational or cerebral point that a promise is exactly the same whether verbal or written. Some feel, 'My word is apparently not good enough'; or, 'they want to have something to hold against me'. Some feel that a dictated form of words is somehow threatening; it is not a personal expression of a state of conscience. Most perhaps feel that it adds a further dimension of pressure from outside on two people whose chief concern is to love one another.

[15]*One in Christ*, IX, 1973, p. 200.
[16]*One in Christ*, VIII, 1972, p. 425.

Canon 1126 of the new Code, quoted above, leaves episcopal conferences entirely free to decide how the matter of the declaration and promise is to be handled. The Directory of the English and Welsh bishops, *Mixed Marriages* (1977), allows parish priests to give the dispensation/permission to marry, but requires that the Catholic party should

> sign the following declaration and promise (preferably in the presence of the non-Catholic):
> I declare that I am ready, as God's law demands, to preserve my Catholic faith and to avoid all dangers of falling away from it. Moreover I sincerely undertake that I will, as God's law also requires, do all in my power to have all the children of our marriage baptized and brought up in the Catholic Church.

It should be noted that the form of words prescribed does not use the word 'promise' but says 'undertake'. This change was made after consultation with Anglicans and others who stressed that the word 'promise' in English almost inevitably conveyed the idea that the person was promising that the children *would* be baptized and brought up as Catholics, even though the bishops in the Directory stressed that

> the content of the promise has changed from what was required before this *Motu Proprio* (Apostolic Letter *Matrimonia Mixta*). It is now a sincere and deliberate undertaking to 'do all in one's power', that is to say, 'all one can do in the actual circumstances of the marriage', 'within the unity of the marriage'. For the reasons we spoke of in commenting on (1) the legal requirement now stops short of the assertion that the Catholic baptism and education of the children will be achieved.

In view of these official glosses on 'do all in my power', it seems fair comment that 'do all in my power' is stronger than the Latin of the Code, *se omnia pro viribus facturam esse*, and that this would more fairly have been translated in the official English version of the Code as 'do all I can'.

The Directory, however requires that the promise be signed by the Catholic, and that the priest send a form to the chancery attesting that this has been done. It would be perfectly possible, and is done in some other countries, that in sending details of the marriage to the chancery the priest handling the marriage should attest that satisfactory undertakings have been given by the Catholic party, without any particular form of words being prescribed, and without the Catholic having to sign anything. This would make an enormous difference both to the priest and to the couple.

The marriage ceremony

The decree *Ne Temere* of 1907, subsequently incorporated into the code of canon law, lays down that for the validity of a Catholic's marriage it must be celebrated (bride and bridegroom are the ministers of the sacrament) in the presence of an authorized priest and two witnesses. This is called the 'canonical form' of the marriage. The law came in, not with mixed marriages in view, but to prevent clandestine marriages. But it has repercussions on mixed marriages: for example, if a Catholic marries an Anglican in an Anglican church without a dispensation from the law of canonical form, the marriage is invalid, not because it took place in an Anglican church or before an Anglican minister: it would have been invalid in a registry office or anywhere else; whereas the marriage of non-Catholic Christians in their own churches or in a registry office is valid Christian marriage by canon law, as they are not bound by the canonical form. (The law of canonical form in fact says nothing about the place at all: a church is obviously the appropriate place, but civil law enters into the determination of possible places.) The purpose of the law of canonical form and the situation created by it is frequently misunderstood by non-Catholics.

Some have questioned the right of the Catholic Church to introduce such a law ruling a marriage *invalid* (no marriage) and not merely illicit. A marriage contracted by two baptized Christians, they say, *must* be a Christian marriage. The matter is only mentioned here in order to note a further difference about marriage. To go into it properly would involve discussing what 'valid' means. At least it means that the Catholic Church does not recognize the marriage as a sacrament, and therefore not as a marriage.[17] And the church must be able to define the conditions for the administration of the sacraments. There used to be a law excommunicating a Catholic who married before a non-Catholic minister, for this was seen as a public act of breaking with the Catholic Church. This has been repealed. However, such Catholics are still not admitted to holy communion, not because of marrying in another Christian church, but because publicly living in a marriage relationship with someone to whom they are not married, and thereby ex-communicating themselves (it means cutting themselves off from holy communion) on moral grounds.

A few years ago it was unheard of for a Catholic to get a dispensation from canonical form so as to be married in the church of his or her partner. Between the papal directives of 1966 and 1970 requests had to go to Rome (so that Rome could be in touch with and assess the general mood in the church), but since *Matrimonia Mixta* bishops can dispense from canonical form themselves and that is now incorporated in the new Code.

An initial practice of doing so only when the non-Catholic was closely related to a minister of his or her church proved unworkable, as it unintentionally brought in a class distinction: it is the middle-class who are related to ordained ministers. The result has been that the practice has become increasingly common, the church of the bride more and more becoming the one in which the wedding takes place. (There is theological sense in this, in that, in the wedding ceremony, the bridegroom represents Christ, and the bride the church.) The Code (Can. 1127.2) says that, 'if serious difficulties stand in the way of observing the canonical form', bishops have the right to dispense from it. This is somewhat cagey and accounts for a tentative development in what is a new field of experience. But, if one looks at the matter more positively, improvement of relationship between the churches itself constitutes a serious ground for dispensation, and no doubt accounts more than any other reason for the gradual growth of the practice. The South African and Canadian episcopal

[17]Indeed, it is hard to see how the word can mean anything *more* than this, when the new Code enacts (Can. 1127.1) that, when a Catholic marries a Christian of eastern rite, the 'canonical form' is only required for liceity and not for validity.

directories expressly give this reason, and add as a further one the pastoral good of the whole marriage and the tranquillity of family relationships.[18] There is no doubt that marriage in a non-Catholic church helps to ease any tensions that may have arisen from the Catholic requirement of a promise about the children.

The second and third reports of the joint Anglican/Roman-Catholic commission on marriage went further and recommended, that is, from both sides, that, 'on condition that joint pastoral preparation has been given, and freedom to marry established to the satisfaction of the bishop of the Roman Catholic party and of the competent Anglican authority, the marriage may validly and lawfully take place before the duly authorized minister of the church of either party'. Two reasons are given: 'First, it is preferable for any practice to be brought within the general law rather than be made the object of frequent dispensation. Secondly, to extend the scope of canonical form to include Anglican ministers celebrating the Anglican rite would be an ecumenical act of profound significance, giving notable substance to those official utterances which, in various ways, have declared a "special relationship" to exist between our two churches.'[19] The suggestion, then, does not amount to an abolition of the law of canonical form between Catholics and Anglicans (for then their marriage in a registry office would have to be recognized as valid), but is that Anglican ministers should be included in the law. Though the second report was produced in 1968 and the third in 1971, there has still been no official reaction from Rome. The reason for the silence cannot be any complications with eastern churches, for what is proposed would bring Roman-Anglican practice into line with what already obtains between Rome and the Eastern churches: for a marriage between a Catholic (Latin or Eastern) and an Eastern non-Catholic (orthodox or even heretical), the presence of a sacred minister of either church is required for validity.[20] Nor can the

[18]*One in Christ*, Vol VII, 1971, p. 227.
[19]Ibid., Vol IX, 1973, pp. 201–202. For the 'special relationship' see *Unitatis Redintegratio* (the Decree on Ecumenism), 13, and Pope Paul's address at the Canonization of the Forty Martyrs.
[20]Code, can. 1127.1.

difficulty be that Catholics would 'skip off' and marry in Anglican churches, for the recommendation puts joint pastoral care as a condition, which Anglican clergy would certainly honour; the need for permission to marry, and the annexed promises, could continue on the Catholic side, and Anglican priests would not solemnize a marriage considered illicit by the Catholic Church.

If, with dispensation from canonical form, the marriage takes place in an Anglican or Protestant church, there is no legal necessity for a Catholic priest to appear or to take any part. It is a pastoral question, to be decided in the concrete circumstances whether he should or not. If he does, it manifests the concord of the churches and helps the Catholic 'side'. If he does not, it manifests full acceptance by the Catholic Church of the ceremony of the other church. At present, in the fairly novel experience of interchange, it seems that the former practice is the more common. It is arguable that the latter is more advanced ecumenically. For the same reason one may question the suggestion, made in some episcopal directories, of working out joint and agreed 'ecumenical marriage rites'. It may well be better that each should accept the other's marriage rite.

If the marriage takes place in a Catholic church, a nuptial mass is permitted by the bishops of England and Wales, whenever the non-Catholic is baptized, and when the priest judges this appropriate.[21] The point of the latter qualification is that it is precisely in the true interchurch marriage that the nuptial mass causes great difficulties. First, it makes the wedding even more unfamiliar to the family of the non-Catholic who, particularly if they are active Christians, may even sense something like a Catholic take-over. It is a delicate point, to which Catholics about to marry are not always very sensitive. Secondly, and more seriously, it creates extreme difficulties about holy communion. According to present ruling, either the Catholic will communicate alone, or neither will; and there is nothing to prevent members of the Catholic side coming up to receive holy communion. Either situation seems intolerable at the centre of a sacrament of love and

[21]Directory, comment on Norm. 11.

union between bride and bridegroom. Hence many priests find
it necessary to dissuade the Catholic party from a nuptial mass
when the other party is a committed member of his or her own
church. The matter can be partly solved by admission of the
non-Catholic to holy communion (on the usual condition of
having a eucharistic faith not inconsistent with Catholic
belief), as has been allowed in Holland since 1966 and in some
dioceses outside Holland since then. But, though a considerable advance, this is not a complete solution from the
churches' point of view: if the Catholic is never to be able to
receive communion in the non-Catholic's church, the invita-
tion at the nuptial mass remains one-sided and could be
interpreted as proselytizing. And what about other non-
Catholics present at the wedding?

The various parts of the new marriage rite lend themselves
to participation by the minister and relatives of the non-
Catholic side, more so when celebrated on its own and apart
from a nuptial mass: words of welcome, scripture reading,
responsorial psalm, address, possibly the ring ceremony,
bidding prayers, concluding ritual and blessing, all offer
opportunities. All participation by the non-Catholic side, even
to get one of them to be at the altar as server, helps them to
experience the ceremony as their own.

Joint pastoral care

Matrimonia Mixta took a big step forward in advocating joint
pastoral care of the couple by the clergy of both churches
(para. d and Norm 14), and the desirability of this is stressed in
the Directory of the English and Welsh Bishops. In 1971 the
Joint Working Group of the British Council of Churches and
the Roman Catholic Church produced a pamphlet of recom-
mendations on the subject aimed to assist clergy in exploring
the idea.[22]

The ability of clergy to co-operate in guiding an interchurch
couple before their marriage will clearly depend on their

[22]*Joint Pastoral Care of Interchurch Marriages*, obtainable from the British
Council of Churches, and printed in full in *One in Christ*, Vol VII, 1971, pp.
235–254.

already existing relationship and on wider fields of co-operation. It is also affected by whether the couple live in the same area or in different ones. The ideal form of co-operation would be for the couple to see both ministers together, even in a foursome, to demonstrate the openness on both sides. If they come to the parish priest first, he should do what he can to see that the non-Catholic goes to his or her own minister. This may seem unrealistic if the non-Catholic has not been in contact with any church or any minister for a long time, but even so, some effort in this direction is not out of place. Every aspect of preparation for marriage, from the basic Christian theology of marriage to details about the service, can be the subject of such joint pastoral guidance. And often the clergy can help the couple with their own relatives, if these are distressed at the marriage and in need of reconciliation with either or both of the partners, and perhaps exerting pressures on them that make their own search for harmony in the religious field more difficult.

Joint pastoral care is not necessarily only a matter for clergy. The experienced and thoughtful interchurch couple can often be a great help to a younger pair preparing for marriage, especially in understanding the problems that will arise and the means of solving them. Some wider schemes have been tried in different parts of the world, notably in Canada, and these include joint publication by the churches of booklets to advise interchurch couples. In Liverpool, a pre-marriage guidance course specifically for mixed marriages has taken place, to cover the many relevant and important areas that ordinary pre-marriage guidance does not treat. In England and Wales there has existed for some years a self-formed Association of Interchurch Families, which meets for an annual week-end conference, and at regional group meetings during the year, and to these events both engaged and married couples come. A parallel association has started in Dublin, and in Northern Ireland.

Joint prayer

The two-church couple can discover and create unity for themselves and their children if they pray at home, whereas there will always be something less than 'full communion' in their public worship. Hence home prayer is more important for them than for the one-church family, both the adult prayer of man and wife and family prayer with the children. It needs effort, of course, but will bring corresponding rewards, particularly as the couple will be finding their own way of praying together and sharing their spiritual heritages, rather than trying to follow received patterns. The recurring decisions that have to be made about the religious life of the family will thus be moulded and carried by an habitual context of their seeking God's guidance together. Family prayers and homespun liturgies – for particular occasions (such as Sunday dinner), particular times of the year, the entertainment of friends, a house group meeting – require ingenuity and imagination, and call on all the talents of celebration, musical, artistic, literary, dramatic. Nowadays there is a lot of useful literature to help. A broad base of home prayer is far and away the most important way in which the couple can fulfil jointly their joint responsibility for the religious upbringing of their children. Even out of a two-church context we are all coming to realize (led chiefly by primary-school teachers) that religious education cannot begin with 'information', instruction of the mind: on the contrary, experience of God's self-giving in the realities of everyday life and of everyday Christian worship must come first, before it can be meaningfully formulated as 'beliefs'. Further, united home religion as an accepted part of family life enables both parents and children to experience unity as coming first, as putting division into perspective, and as being deep and strong enough to sustain within itself necessary differences of religious conviction; these, on such a basis, can then be made into creative rather than divisive tensions. That, of course, requires effort too. But how well worth while! For it is precisely at this point, and in this way, that the two-church family can be a sign of, and a force for, true ecumenism within the couple's churches and in their locality.

The older type of mixed marriage, in which the non-Catholic partner (usually husband) at most accompanies the family to Sunday mass, is still far and away the commonest. If the Catholic (wife) has never really tried to share the partner's tradition of Christian thought and public worship, it is hardly surprising if the non-Catholic almost or wholly opts out of the religious life of the family – indeed, opts out of religious life, leaving this to the others (woman and children). The whole tenor of *Matrimonia Mixta* is against either partner opting out, and heralds a new age for the interchurch marriages of Catholics. It is Catholics far more than others who need to take the initiative, Catholics who need urging and convincing that, from engagement onwards, they should belong as fully as possible to the church of their partner, if he is in any true sense to belong to theirs. (This is the right way, and the only right way today, to present Catholicism as a church which other Christians might some day want to join.[23] Hence from the start couples are going to have to form their programme of public worship (both every Sunday, or yours this week and mine next?), which will have to be modified in the developing situations of baby-minding, young children, children of varying ages. When they are young, the children will take for granted and as normal whatever their parents decide about church-going, and *a priori* fears about 'confusing the children' have been shown by experience to be illusory. When they are teenagers, well, there is a lot of sense in one grandparent's remark: 'We should be very relieved if they go to any church at all'. There is at least as much likelihood that they will develop their own church-going life, if they have been brought up to know two church traditions, even if they know they fully belong to only one, than if they have been kept exclusively in one.

Baptism

Apart from 'the promises', there is nothing more acutely difficult for the inter-church couple than baptism. Particularly if they have done everything possible to be and to live as a united 'domestic church', as *Lumen Gentium* (n. 11) calls the family. There is a very great deal one can do to help them

[23]May I at this point refer to my Catholic Truth Society pamphlet, *Towards Christian Union*, pp. 15–17, for a somewhat fuller treatment of this crucial matter.

make, experience at the time of baptism, and live out in practice, a difficult decision. But one can help them most by enabling them to face the fact, right from the start, that they have a decision to make, which they cannot leave for their children to make for themselves. Most interchurch couples are not particularly 'theological'. Many will feel, perhaps with some vagueness about the details, that they can give their children an experience of the full strength of two traditions living in harmony with each other, and leave them to choose in time for themselves – if the two churches are still divided when that time comes. They will want to fend off the separation of the churches from their own family; they will try to avoid options that suggest that division is going to continue for ever; they will expect their two churches to be at least much closer to each other than they are at the moment, by the time their children get into their teens. And so they will grope for a baptism that is simply 'into Christ', or 'into the one church of Christ', and not one that forces an option. But this is not possible. Why this is so can be explained at various levels. First, and pragmatically, no minister will baptize except into his own communion (except perhaps in one of the rare 'ecumenical parishes'), and certainly not a Catholic priest. Secondly, the couple must look ahead to first communion: if the children are to be prepared (with other children with whom they will 'belong') for communion in the Catholic Church at the age of six or seven, they must first be members of the Catholic Church, and so should be baptized into it in infancy; if for communion in another church at another age, this decision similarly redounds on baptism. So the parents in fact have to take the decision for the children, and must be helped to accept this fact from the outset: it will be harder to form a truly joint decision if its dimensions have not been clearly seen long before the time comes. It is a mistake to start from baptism and to try to solve other questions from there. What is going to matter most to the child is, not the church into which he or she is canonically baptized, but the religious upbringing the parents give – in its general and unitive aspects, but also in particular and in its option aspects. Among these is the fact that the child will soon need to 'belong principally' with other children of the same age, Catholic or Anglican or Protestant.

But thirdly, and more profoundly, there is the nature of baptism itself. It is and must be into a believing community that is aware of itself as such internally, and recognizable as such externally. Certainly, baptism is primarily into Christ's body, as a God-given and heavenly reality that transcends all divisions. Certainly, baptism is also into the one church of Christ as it exists in *visible* unity in human history.[24] And the grasp of these two truths can greatly help an interchurch couple to see the 'divisive option' in perspective, as an option mainly for one church but not to the total exclusion of the other. But the one church that makes visible and active among us the heavenly kingdom of Christ ultimately only exists in partly separated Christian communions.[25] As a mystery of God's self-gift and man's inadequate reception, it simultaneously exists at the three levels of heavenly kingdom, one church, separate churches. The option for baptism is an option at all three levels.

So the couple can be helped in their decision by a grasp of these truths. They can be helped to accept that there remain insurmountable difficulties for interchurch marriage, which can only be solved by the union of the churches, not by themselves. It is within such barriers that they are challenged to live and to work for that union. They can be further very considerably helped, when they have reached their decision about the church of baptism, by the way the baptism is performed. A baptized non-Catholic is already by his or her own baptism in partial or imperfect communion with the Catholic Church. If a parent has agreed to have the child baptized into the Catholic Church, he or she is in far fuller communion with the Catholic Church than the rest of his or her own church, both by marrying a Catholic and by undertaking the responsibility of bringing up the child as a Catholic. It is these facts, and not merely the psychological needs of a Christian parent (which have great importance),

[24]The truth that the historical and actual church is *visibly* united as well as visibly divided (theologically it is united prior to being divided) is of immense importance in any ecclesiology of ecumenism, but cannot be developed here.

[25]This thought does not exclude the idea that the one church of Christ 'subsists' (only exists fully) in one communion.

that need the fullest possible recognition and expression in the baptismal ceremony. It is to be hoped that church authorities will give the fullest consideration to the celebration of baptism into the Catholic Church (no other is here being considered) for interchurch families: not only full participation by the other church, when the child is baptized by a Catholic priest in a Catholic church; but baptism by a Catholic priest in the church of the other partner where the other church can allow this; baptism in the home with a large interchurch gathering, for this may more fully express the actual situation of the family as two-church than a baptism in the church of either partner; and finally baptism by an Anglican or Protestant minister in a Catholic church. When, in any of these situations, the child is entered into the baptismal registers of both churches, this helps the non-Catholic parent very greatly to feel that the child has not been 'taken away'. It has no other theological significance, unless both churches accept the child as a member. And of course it has no here and now significance for the child: what matters to him is how he is brought up.

Communion

The deeper the mutual Christian involvement of the couple becomes, the more will they develop and experience the need to receive communion together; and parents with their children. Intercommunion is a very complex topic, and the more one thinks about it the more one realizes that the main arguments both for and against are all good arguments – and do not cancel each other out. However, if one is focussing on interchurch marriages, it needs to be realized that one is not considering the total relationships between churches, but the profound and lifelong Christian communion of a small and clearly distinguishable number of individuals, who are each firmly in communion with their own churches and intend to remain so: individuals, furthermore, who are more deeply committed than anyone else can claim to be to the union of the churches.

The Free Churches have long invited other committed Christians to share their eucharistic communion. In 1972, the

Church of England 'admitted to the holy communion . . . baptized persons who are communicant members of other churches which subscribe to the doctrine of the holy Trinity' (Canon B, 15A). About the same time, official developments for interchurch couples began in the Catholic Church with the issue by the Secretariat for Promoting Christian Unity of an instruction (approved by the Pope) on admission to communion in the Catholic Church in particular cases.[26] No mention is made in this instruction of interchurch families as possible cases, but it brings out two points: that exceptions to the general rule that ties eucharistic to ecclesial communion depend on situations of serious *spiritual* need and not on merely dramatic physical circumstances (concentration camps etc.); and that rulings for particular cases cannot come from above, but must be and are in the hands of the local bishops or episcopal conference. (In addition to being in serious spiritual need, the non-Catholic should take the initiative in asking, and should have a eucharistic faith not incompatible with Catholic belief.) The reason why the interchurch family can be considered under this heading is that, the more profound their joint Christian commitment, the greater will be their spiritual need to communicate together *as a family*; and from this they are at the moment barred in the Catholic Church's general rules.

Since the publication of this instruction much has happened in various parts of the world about this question of admission of the non-Catholic partner to communion. It is all fully documented in a book published in 1983, *Sharing Communion*,[27] which mainly consists of the experience and views of the inter-church couples themselves. In a conclusion to the book I argue that local bishops have both the right to admit the non-Catholic partner to communion, and the responsibility of deciding the matter; i.e. it does not rest with 'higher authority'.

It would falsify the facts if, at the end, the impression was left that inter-church couples are in any way a 'precious' group, or in any unacceptable sense a pressure group. They do

[26]Text in *One in Christ*, Vol VIII, 1972, pp. 393–398. Text of a further 'interpretative note' on the Instruction, ibid., Vol X, 1974.
[27]*Sharing Communion*, ed., Ruth Reardon and Melanie Finch, Collins 1983.

not want to be regarded as chosen souls, or even as exceptional. They do not experience their humanity, their Christianity or their marriage that way. They wish only to be understood and accepted for what they are. It is rather their churches than themselves who tend to regard them as odd, extraordinary, special, not quite fitting in. True inter-church marriages involving Catholics are still comparatively rare, because the Catholic Church has only recently made them possible. If they were sympathetically understood and cared for among existing mixed marriages, and without increasing these, they could become quite common, i.e. many 'merely mixed' marriages would be encouraged to become true interchurch marriages.

6

EUCHARISTIC BELIEF[1]

The replies of some couples to the questionnaire on eucharistic belief and practice[2] raise the question how far people are *misunderstanding* each other, or the doctrine of their own church, rather than *disagreeing*. Hence these paragraphs offer an attempt at clarification of 'real presence' and of 'sacrifice'.

The body of the Lord

Paul is the clue to the meaning of 'body' (*soma*) in the New Testament. He did not think in the Greek way of distinguishing one reality completely from another: e.g. body/soul. (And you cannot distinguish body and blood in that way as the body includes the blood.) Paul's Hebraic way of thinking was in wholes or areas of experience. I experience my *self* as a body (Well, I do don't I?). 'Body' is not the 'I' that experiences but the 'me' that I experience. I experience my body-self as 'flesh', i.e. fragile, mortal, subject to death, to law, to sin. But I also experience my body-self as 'spirit' i.e. open to the action of God.

There is no 'is' (copula) in Aramaic. Jesus said: This my body-self given (broken) for you; this my blood (i.e. life) poured out for you. Blood was thought of as conveying God's gift of life, which is why Jews do not eat meat without first draining the blood. So Jesus was not distinguishing body from

[1] Written for the Association of Interchurch Families.
[2] Now published as *Sharing Communion: an Appeal to the Churches*, Collins 1983.

blood, but uttering parallel sayings as was common in his language and culture.

It is certain that Christian belief always was that it is the *risen* Jesus, the Lord (the title is always and only used of the risen Christ), who is present and is received in the eucharist. When Paul says, 'You proclaim the death of the Lord until he comes' (I Cor. 11.26), he is not saying that they proclaim the death of the mortal Jesus, but the death of the risen Christ: he is holding cross and resurrection together in one. And 'the Lord' is the risen Jesus who pours out on us the Spirit he has received from his Father, the life-force of God.

The Corinthians had over-materialistic ideas of resurrection. Paul takes up most of I Cor. 15 dispelling them and wrestling with the difficulties of finding adequate language to speak of the risen Christ. Flesh-body does not rise. The Lord is spirit-body (this would be a contradiction in terms to a Greek thinker). He even says, 'the Lord is spirit'; but it is *the Lord* who is spirit, the risen Jesus. Jesus does not cease to be a man (cease to be incarnate) by being risen, exalted, glorified. He experiences himself as fully spirit-self or spirit-body. He gives himself to us as spirit-body.

Really present in and for receiving

The eucharistic belief witnessed in the New Testament is that the bread and wine are the risen body-self of Christ *in the receiving*. If you read the eucharistic texts of the New Testament carefully (Paul and John), you will find that there is no evidence for any further or more developed belief. This is already a very great deal.

This is called 'receptionism' and most Christians hold at least this belief. It was the belief of Calvin. Zwingli taught that the bread and wine were not more than symbols of the Lord's reality. Some individual Christians may not go further than this belief, but as far as I know it is not the doctrine of any main Christian communion.

By the third century the conviction had taken hold in both East and West that, if the bread and wine were the risen body of Christ *in* the receiving, and could be carried to the sick and imprisoned for communion, they must already have become the body of Christ *for* the receiving. There had been a mysterious change of the elements. It is noteworthy that this doctrine prevailed in the church without argument and remained unchallenged until the eleventh century. It is the doctrine endorsed by The Anglican Roman Catholic International Commission (ARCIC). When it was challenged, this was because the fact had been lost sight of that it was the risen, not simply the crucified, Lord who was present and was received, and very crude and distasteful flesh-language was being used.

Language

That is really all there is to say about belief and doctrine in regard to real presence. All the rest is a matter of language in which to express *that* belief in a mysterious change. Not a matter of more belief or extra doctrine.

There is no adequate language to express a mysterious change, because it is not the same as any of the situations from which language can be drawn. It is best to coin a new word and to stick to it. The presence of Christ is a sacramental presence, a mystery presence, the presence of the mystery of the risen Christ. Other language misleads.

The language of Aristotle was introduced to *spiritualize* what had become crude. Unfortunately that language in turn came to have a mechanistic flavour. The language of the church was 'reality' and 'appearance': the reality of the bread and wine changes, the appearance does not. The language of Aristotle was 'substance' and 'accident' and introduced a refinement: the substance of the bread is changed but the accidents not, so the whole reality is not changed: trans-substantiation ('ss' please!) But of course in aristotelianism 'substance' meant metaphysical substance. And who understands that now? Certainly not the ordinary lay Catholic who may insist on the use of the word. And among those who do understand it many reject the implication of a misguided metaphysic or attempt to understand the constituents of reality.

The philosophy of Aristotle was never imposed as necessary to eucharistic doctrine. What Trent said was that the change of the reality (substance) of the bread and wine into the reality (substance) of the body and blood of Christ, while the appearances of bread and wine remained, was *appropriately called* by the church 'trans-substantiation'. It is a remark about language. Seen as appropriate then, the language has ceased to be appropriate for three reasons: because people no longer understand the philosophical system to which it is attached; because it acquired a mechanistic flavour; and because at Trent 'body' and 'blood' were being understood in the Greek and not the Hebraic sense. As ARCIC rightly says, and rightly puts in a footnote, the language does not purport to show *how* the mysterious change takes place.

The sad thing today is that Catholics who no longer know what the word means often say that 'they' (i.e. other Christians) do not accept trans-substantiation, and jump from there to imagining that 'they' do not believe they are receiving the body of Christ. They do. If they reject the language, this is because it seems to be trying to explain the change in terms of a philosophy of nature and so to de-mystify it and make it mechanistic.

Personally present

Other troubles are caused by other words. The ciborium is physically present in the tabernacle, but the body of Christ is not present in that way, i.e. not physically present. If the word is to retain any sense at all, it should be kept for the proper field of physics: a presence detectable by natural vision and natural sciences. Paul insisted that the risen body-self was not a physical (natural)-body, but a spirit-body: I Cor. 15.44. Flesh and blood, i.e. the flesh-body-self which is buried in the ground, do not inherit the kingdom.

'Corporal' presence causes further and similar trouble. It is the body (*corpus*) of Christ which is present, so the word seems at first sight appropriate. But it is the spirit-body-self of the risen Christ that is mysteriously present. Just stick to 'sacramentally present'!

One trouble about attempts to insist on realistic language is that one inevitably finds oneself treating 'the body of Christ' as a thing: really, objectively, there, present, regardless of any personal relationship. It is not our faith that makes Christ the Lord present. But the risen Lord is personally present as a gift of his spirit-self to us. He is not effectively present *to* us until we recognize and respond to his presence in faith.

You are the body of Christ

ARCIC is a bit light on reservation of the elements for communion to the sick, and on the veneration, adoration, of Christ present and devotions to the reserved sacrament. The place to start is with meditation on the mysterious unity of eucharist and church. The ruthless Western mind came to make distinctions which were unheard of in the first eight or nine centuries and lost a good deal in the process.

First and foremost it is we who are the body of Christ, we the baptized community. We are communion (*koinonia*). Only we can celebrate the eucharist and nourish the life already given us of the body of Christ. The eucharist is a concentrated or crystallized expression of what we are all the time. If we think of the reserved sacrament as the abiding sacrament of *Christ's abiding presence in us*, his body, the different practices become intelligible. Certainly, the elements were at first reserved solely for communion to those unable to be present at the celebration. But, with a fuller understanding of both church and eucharist as communion, the reserved elements can rightly be seen as a focus for the church's daily, unceasing, life and prayer.

Sacrifice

Then there's sacrifice. This is a less difficult area for a couple who want to receive communion together, but it is within the field of eucharistic belief about which they would like to be able to agree.

At the Reformation the Protestants objected to chantry masses etc. and cut the ground from under them by asserting that the eucharist was not a sacrifice. The Catholics were sure it was but did not have any clear idea how it was. There was no received theology of the mass as sacrifice: Thomas Aquinas had said nothing about it, as he never got to that part of his

Summa. Since then various Catholic theologies of the eucharist as sacrifice have developed. None of them is mandatory or 'the' Catholic theology of sacrifice. Trent said a certain amount, but it can fit into various theologies.

One argument has been futile: is it a sacrifice or is it a meal? There are many different kinds of sacrifice but they are all meals. Sometimes the meal is wholly God's (holocaust) and it is all put on his table: an altar is God's table. Sometimes they are shared with God: his part is put on his table (perhaps burned there, perhaps carried off as the priests' portion), and we take our part to eat at our table at home. Sometimes God shares our table at home (any Jewish sabbath meal).

Whether the last supper was the Passover meal or not, and for this purpose it does not matter, it was certainly a ritual meal of some kind, and so a sacrifice. And the eucharist is certainly a ritual meal, a meal shared with God, and so a sacrifice. What is shared? Precisely the risen-body-self of Christ. So it is a communion sacrifice, a sacrifice because it is communion. More technically, a sacramental sacrifice or a sacrificial sacrament. Not a sacrifice plus a sacrament, so that for example the priest offers a sacrifice and we others may or may not communicate in it. We only participate fully in a communion sacrifice by communicating. The priest must communicate and only celebrates this sort of sacrifice by doing so.

One can go further in constructing a theology of sacrifice, and it is then the trouble starts. But I would suggest one doesn't have to go further. The church lived the eucharist for centuries without drawing out all the theology. Indeed, has it done so yet? The point is really to do it, to share it. Which is what Jesus told us to do.

Offered

The 'trouble does not stem from eucharistic theology at all but from theologies of salvation (redemption, atonement). At the time of the Reformation both Catholics and Reformers were limited by the view that we are saved by an event in past history, the self-sacrifice of Jesus on the cross. The resurrection was not regarded as an essential part of the saving work of

Jesus but as God's reward to him. Some evangelicals today still wish to assert this (and ARCIC wobbles). And in that perspective it is extremely hard to see how the eucharist could be a repeated series of sacrificial acts without adding to the self-sacrifice of Jesus, or suggesting it was incomplete or inadequate. Catholic theologies of the making present today of a past act in history, so that we can participate in it rather than add to it, are not entirely convincing.

But once you see that the resurrection, the risen-ness of Jesus and his sharing fully the life and power of his Father, is an integral part of his redeeming, atoning, saving work, and so of his sacrifice, then everything falls into place. The risen-ness of Jesus, his being 'at the right hand of God' (seated on God's throne and sharing God's power with us, is what the image conveys), is not an event in past history; it is not in history at all, but outside history in God's eternity. The risen Lord gives us the eternal life he draws from the Father in baptism, in the eucharist etc.

Now we can say (as the epistle to the Hebrews keeps saying) that the sacrifice of Christ is an event that starts in time but is completed in eternity. Not a once-and-for-all past event. But an outside-time event and therefore once and for all.

Then we can say that in the eucharist Christ gathers us, in all times and places, into his eternal sacrifice so that we 'enter into the movement of his self-offering'. The latter is what ARCIC says. But it is rather roundabout, and has the danger of making 'we' the subject of the sentence. If Christ were always the subject of the sentence, the difficulties would evaporate. *Not* 'we offer' or 'we enter'. *Not* 'the church offers', though that is all right if you always understand by 'the church', not us apart from Christ, but the risen Lord present and active in his people. *But* in the eucharist, precisely as communion, Christ gathers us daily and everywhere into his eternal self-offering. He is always living to make intercession for us.

PART II

RECONCILING MAN WITH GOD

7

SPIRITUAL HEALTH

The Old Testament

To the Hebraic mind health is a part of life, which is a divine gift. The one Spirit of God is the source of all life. Hence there is no counterpart in Hebrew for the word 'health', nor is there consideration in the Old Testament of natural life as such; there is very little advertence to physical remedies. Sickness is a diminution of life, a withdrawal of God's gift or Spirit.

Sickness and death thus constitute a continuum, and the whole is a punishment for sin. Hence in sickness there must first be repentance for sin and prayer to God for deliverance. The idea is reflected in the epistle of James: 'The prayer of faith will save the sick man, and the Lord will raise him up; and if he has committed sins they will be forgiven. Therefore confess your sins to one another, and pray for one another, that you may be healed' (5.15–16).

The later layers of the Old Testament reflect the rise of angelology and demonology in Jewish thought: the forces assisting man or assailing him are personified as angels and demons; prayer in sickness is for liberation from demons, i.e. from the powers of evil. This background is shared by New Testament writers: for Paul death is man's 'last enemy' (I Cor. 15.26).

The speculation of rabbis in late Judaism tried to calculate more exactly, and to ascribe particular illnesses to particular sins: for instance, quinsy was thought to be the result of not paying one's tithes!

The New Testament

The New Testament retains the single or integrated vision of man as a whole, for good or for ill. Jesus' miracles are a sign of the coming kingdom, i.e. the coming total salvation of man, including freedom from ills. For Paul, 'flesh' is man's whole this-worldly condition, in which he is subject to the law, to sin, to sickness and death: the three are interlocked as aspects of a single reality, rather than related to each other as cause and effect. The saving effects of baptism and the eucharist are understood in a quasi-magical way as including bodily health: 'He who eats and drinks, eats and drinks judgment on himself if he does not discern the Body. That is why many of you are feeble and sick and a number have died' (I Cor. 11.29–30).

The synoptic gospels all see Jesus' miracles as signs of the kingdom, but variously. For Mark, Jesus' powers are a frontal attack on the realm of Satan. Matthew brings out that the miracles are a realization of the Old Testament promises of salvation. In Luke they show the power of the Spirit given to Jesus to equip him for his ministry; they are pointers to his future Lordship (full share in God's power over all cosmic forces) when he is risen and exalted. Thus there is little or no distinction between sickness and diabolic attack.

Hence there is a double meaning to the phrase 'your faith has saved you'; reliance on Jesus brings relief from suffering: true faith in him brings ultimate salvation. The phrase, used once each by Matthew and Mark, occurs four times in Luke (the doctor), three times of cures, and once (7.50) of the woman who was a sinner.

Two main features stand out from the general biblical understanding of health. First, bodily and spiritual health are one: they are integrated in a view of man's personal relationship with God: the characteristic greeting, *shalom*, is a prayer for the total well-being of God's favour. And, secondly, this global health or integrity is seen as dependent on an outside source, the Spirit of God.

Hellenic influence

This integrated view broke up in Christianity and in Europe under the impact of Greek thought. In Greek there are words for physical health, and this was understood as a balance or harmony of internal forces, such as would equip a man to perform essential or desired tasks. In the *Republic* Plato extended the idea to the mental forces or powers of the soul.

But the chief impact of hellenic thought came from the distinction between body and soul. The distinction tended to become a dichotomy, as the 'true man' or real man came to be regarded as the soul, and the body as a regrettable appendage. For the Stoics, physical health was in itself a matter of indifference and could be an evil in so far as it was allowed to impair the right use of reason. Socrates in the *Phaedo* chides his disciples for grief at his coming death: they should rejoice that his soul was about to be released and disentangled from the body, and thereby become free to contemplate eternal reality; this is what he had tried to train them to do in this life, as true philosophers.

The dichotomy had incalculable effects on Christian spirituality. It leads us to imagine our 'true selves' as some kind of lightsome angelic being, caught in the murky toils of the body. Ignatius Loyola in the *Spiritual Exercises* (n. 47) summons us to an effort of imagination, 'that my soul is a prisoner in this corruptible body'. Longing for the vision of God, as intellectual contemplation, is Platonism or Plotinianism in Christian dress. The doctrine that the soul is inherently or naturally immortal is in the last resort a blatant contradiction of the gospel, which proclaims the salvation of the whole man (indeed of all creation) and at the same time gives him no hope for survival except in and through the resurrection of Christ. See I Cor. 15.12–19 and Rom. 8.9–23, especially: 'He who raised Christ Jesus from the dead will give life to your mortal bodies also through his Spirit which dwells in you'.

The body came to be regarded as at best 'the instrument of the soul': this is only half way to the Christian task of integrating the whole person into the body of Christ. In the Renaissance and the modern period an individualistic note was added, and 'my spiritual life' was to be cultivated, with contempt for the body. Spiritual health could be unrealistically regarded as independent of bodily health, and perhaps dangerously regarded as independent of what we would call mental health.

Where are we today?

We all experience some uncertainty about where to go next, when traditionally accepted categories are seen to be inadequate. There are no very clear answers to the questions that arise. All that will be attempted here is to give some few pointers towards further reflection.

1. Alongside the body-soul dichotomy, there developed in Western thought a mechanical view of nature. Nature was studied as a timeless machine, an intricate mechanism; the cause-effect relationship of the parts and sub-parts could be ever more exactly charted. Medicine as a science could only be 'physical medicine'. At least until Darwin the perspective of growth and development in nature was lacking. Growth in perfection or 'supernatural growth', was allowed to the soul in its relation to God, but the idea of spiritual growth could not be integrated into an understanding of the growth of the human as a whole.

Hence, whereas the biblical view of sickness virtually ignores physical remedies, the independent scientific view that emerged ignored the wholeness of the person. The concept of psycho-somatic illness, and with it the return to an integral view of the human being, is a very recent one.

2. On the other hand, we need some conceptual apparatus for dealing with the more bodily and the more spiritual or mental elements of ourselves. We could be helped by the Hebraic view of man as an animated body, not as an incarnate soul; a view that starts from our experience of ourselves as bodily beings. We have to acknowledge the polarity that exists in our selves without making it a dualism or a disjunction.

More importantly, we have to deal in practice and in life with these two poles of our selves and integrate them: the spirit can become 'fleshly' or materialized, by concentration on comfort and pleasure; the bodily powers can be spiritualized by integration into the purposes of the spirit.

This seems to imply a process of growth or maturing. Hence 'spiritual health' may not be a very helpful concept, in that it implies a normal level of functioning that is to be maintained, rather than a goal to be reached after growth.

3. The considerations so far advanced do not take into account the social dimensions of health, the interdependence of individual and community. The Old Testament had a corporate view of salvation; this underlies the New Testament, which proclaimed a kingdom, a true people of God, a unity in the body of Christ. Christian theology, after a period of individualism, has returned to a consideration of the mutual conditioning of individual and society. We have to ask how the spiritual health of the individual depends on that of the society in which he lives.

4. May there not be some truth in the biblical view that the integration of a human being must come from a point outside, that in contrast to the Hellenic view of health as a balance of internal forces, it must always be arbitrary for each person to take any point within their own components, any point within their own life and experience, as one from which they can integrate or give meaning and direction to the whole? Modern men and women lack any standpoint outside themselves from which to achieve an integrated view of themselves and the world.[1]

5. In an article entitled 'Healing and the Divided Self'[2] Father Michael Ivens notes two conflicting spiritualities. In the spirituality of patience, there is awareness of the need to turn to psychiatric medicine for help; there is no real hope of a cure; there is stress on the need to live with disability, and on the possibility of holiness without wholeness if the weakness is personally related to God. The spirituality of power insists that bringing to wholeness is a basic part of the Christian ministry; there is stress on the importance of the praying, supporting, mediating group. Instead of being set against each

[1]Cf. John S. Dunne, *A Search for God in Time and Memory*, Sheldon Press 1975.
[2]*The Way*, July 1976.

other these two approaches should, rather, be seen as complementary, each compensating for the partiality and possible dangers of the other. Peace may then become the context of healing.

8

THEOLOGY OF SIN

Modern theologies of sin

Today theologies of sin abound, and this section will try to sketch some of them. Their one common and overriding feature is to insist that we do not first understand sin, and then salvation (or redemption, or whatever general word one uses). Sin is a theological and not a merely moral concept. If there were no grace, there would be no sin. It is in knowing God as giving himself to us, transforming us, calling us to share his life, redeeming us in Christ, that we begin to understand sin. Sin is all that opposes salvation. It is not sinners who have a deep sense of sin but saints.

1. The idea of sin develops progressively in the Bible. It is very difficult to generalize in a specialist area, but broadly speaking one may say that in the older layers of the Old Testament God's election comes first: Israel is God's people by his choice, not if and in so far as she obeys cultic and moral commands. Commandments are soon added as man's moral response, but they are simple and easy to keep. Goodness, righteousness, is a quality of God: his covenant love and his faithfulness. Man is righteous because he is an Israelite, faithful to the covenant, trusting in God. Fidelity and infidelity on the part of man are a communal idea, not yet much concerned with moral behaviour. In the history of the monarchy faithfulness to the cult is the test; infidelity is adultery. But the commandments grew in complexity and their codification gave rise to the idea of an external code of behaviour as a measure of what keeping the covenant meant.

The idea of personal guilt was at first too interior and individualistic: sin was thought of as communal and as disturbing an external objective order; an evil act (e.g. killing a man) and its consequences were seen as a single whole and as endangering the community. Priests decided on whether and how sin could be cleansed ritually, to save the community; if it could not be expiated (cleansed), the individual would bear the curse (excommunication, death) to avert it from the people. The dominant idea is of solidarity in righteousness and sin: the sins of one generation are visited on the next. Not till Jeremiah and Ezekiel does the idea of personal responsibility begin to come through. The 'new covenant' proclaims an interior and subjective idea of righteousness. After the Exile the drift towards legalism is greatly accentuated with the growing power of the priests. (Did not this happen again in Christian history?)

So Jesus recalls Israel to its earlier and more basic inspiration: to the centrality of personal relationship with God. It is in knowing God that we know what love is, and therefore what sin is. A new covenant, a new communion of men with God and with each other, is inaugurated.

2. Paul sees man as experiencing himself (his bodily self, *soma*) both as 'flesh' and as 'spirit'. As flesh in that he is assailed by sin and death, which are cosmic and demonic forces of destruction; he knows himself to be fragile, mortal and perishable, threatened by what we would call disintegration, incapable of living up to his ideals and vision. He knows himself as spirit in that he experiences his body-self as open to the conquering, liberating and transforming action of God.

Man-in-Adam (flesh) is involved in the complex of law-sin-death. Man-in-Christ is set free from this complex. He is set free from the law, not just as a set of rules, but as a dispensation governing his relation to God. He is set free from law as code, but not from law as compulsion, as imperative: 'The law of the Spirit of life in Jesus Christ has set me free from the law of sin and death' (Rom. 8.2). But he is under a new compulsion, a new imperative (Rom. 7.5–6): Paul even calls it a new slavery (Rom. 6.15–18). But the Christian is not under a new code: no code could ever free us from sin and death, only the Spirit can do that, for 'where the Spirit of the Lord (the risen Christ) is, there is freedom' (II Cor. 3.17). Christ, not the written *Torah*, is God's Wisdom: his Spirit dwelling in our hearts is the new obligation and driving force (Rom. 8.12–14). That 'law' can never be codified: one can only say that love is the fulfilment of (the) law (Gal. 5.13–14; Rom. 13.8–10).

All the same, there is a code of Christian laws. Paul does not hesitate to promulgate some of them himself. But they do not justify, any more than did the old law. The life of the Spirit does not consist in obeying rules. They are a rough guide to the personal demands of the Spirit, a pedagogue to Christ, a help to the struggling sinner who is not wholly driven by the Spirit.

Augustine, who dealt in moral psychology rather than the metaphysics of nature and grace, took this up with his idea of *gratia liberatrix*: the personal self-gift of God sets me free from rules, from weakness, from disintegration; it creates my freedom.

3. Perhaps the most striking feature of modern theologies of sin is their return to an awareness of the corporate or social dimensions of sin, in reaction against an almost wholly individualistic understanding of sin (and salvation) which prevailed in European moral philosophy and in the development of moral theology: the Old Testament awareness of solidarity in sin and in righteousness is reinstated, but with new content.

This is due to the birth and development of a sense of history, a realization of the degree to which in all ages perceptions of value are culturally and socially conditioned. Indeed, our moral awareness is first a sharing in, a being conditioned by, the moral perceptions of the society into which we are born, and only slowly do personal assimilation, assessment, criticism and innovation emerge. We do not arrive on the scene as fully constituted persons, separate centres of awareness, self-determination and responsibility; we are able to move in that direction only in interaction with the expanding society of persons we encounter and relate to. In so far as we mature as persons, we come to realize that the good and bad in our society can only be developed or changed by corporate opinion and action. Our responsibility is not just for personal integrity, but for changing society. On a theological plane the concept of covenant has received new emphasis: it determines our relationship to God, not as separate individuals, but as a people he has chosen for himself.

4. Within the very general perspective of the previous section one may further reflect on the processes by which we discover and construct our own identity. We need to identify ourselves with the secure and familiar group in order to grow as persons. And inevitably, tragically, in the process we identify ourselves *against* other groups; our family, our village (if it is Cana, can any good come of Nazareth?), our class, our nation, our race. . . . 'That by which we identify ourselves and have our sense of identity, significance and belonging, is that by which we dehumanize others'.[1] There is, perhaps fortuitously, an interesting sequence of us-and-them passages in Luke 9.49–56, in which Jesus breaks through the barriers. God's election and new covenant call and challenge us continually to break out of all our tribalisms, and to accept, respect, and relate more deeply to wider and wider groupings of persons. This is the process of becoming human, in the image of the New Man, Christ – for each of us, and for the human race. It is the building of the kingdom of God, an eschatological goal. 'No one can be fully human until everyone is fully human.'[2]

5. Another obvious feature of modern theologies of grace and sin is that they think in dynamic terms, categories of growth, not in terms of timeless essences and laws. Teilhard de Chardin may have convinced neither the scientists nor the philosophers, but he caught the imagination and responded to the aspiration of a generation by transposing Christian doctrine into the key of growth, development, evolution. The chief dogmatic shift is to see the final kingdom as God's first and only plan, and creation as the 'first step' to its fulfilment. There is only a supernatural order: nature is the material on which God works, and which he transforms. It is the goal, the omega, which explains the alpha and all that lies between. This perspective reinforces that of the solidarity of humanity in sin and salvation.

[1]David Jenkins, *The Contradiction of Christianity*, SCM Press 1976, p. 16.
[2]*The Contradiction of Christianity*, p. 36, 102.

Categories of individual and generic growth, however, raise far-reaching questions about understanding sin. In general, salvation would lie in response to God's call to grow, to break through into new relationships, into deeper inner awareness and outer relation, new appreciation of others' needs, new understanding of prevailing injustices. Sin would lie in selfish clinging to myself as I am (perhaps in preoccupation with my authenticity?), clinging to security in the familiar and in structures that meet my needs. But at the same time, if God has created a human race that is summoned, not to obey timeless natural laws, but to develop, to respond progressively to his transforming grace, it is not blameworthy that we are not at the omega or end-point of his purposes, but only somewhere along the way. Nor am I guilty or blameworthy for the inability to be perfect here and now which involvement in a growth process necessarily entails: only for the degree to which I resist God's transforming and expanding power.

6. Augustine understood man as driven by a divine discontent, restless, searching, always reaching beyond his present into a greater future. Man is made for God, whether he knows it or not, and his inner driving force, which gives him all his creative power, his hunger to know more and more, his artistic talents, his self-transcendence and spirituality, is in fact the force of God's self-communicating love drawing man to himself. Hence the human capacity for both joy and suffering, for love and for hate, for creation and destruction, for hope and despair. In his heights and depths he reaches for and becomes aware of absolutes of the divine and the diabolic, heaven and hell. Here one touches on the deep mystery of good and evil, and human understanding can at best point in the right directions, without encompassing or exhausting. But obscurely one can see that there can be no sin without grace; that the *same* force of God's love gives man the power to create and to destroy, to love and to hate; that God is God and in an ultimate sense is responsible for the human condition; that God is God and does not need vindicating; that talk about God tolerating evil never reaches the heart of the matter.

At a point in history where the options before the human race seem increasingly apocalyptic, where for the first time humanity has the possibility of either total self-destruction or of breaking through into a new 'one world' of interdependence and trust, one is forced to admit that there are no guarantees from within history and the human track-record that he will choose aright. The Christian message then has to be one of hope, one of trust in God's fidelity and the proclamation of the Easter gospel. The victory of Christ does not hang in the balance: it has already been achieved.

7. Out of some of these contexts there arises a distinction between sin and sins. (What John the Baptist said was, 'Behold the Lamb of God, who takes away the *sin* of the world'.) If 'sin' be taken to cover the need the world has and that I have in it for salvation – its frailties, inadequacies, dislocations, distortions, blindness, smallness of heart, in short the distance it falls short of the glory of God – then we are not personally responsible for its givenness, though our inheritance creates manifold responsibilities and opportunities for us. 'Sins' would be our personal contributions, by omission and commission, to the sin of the world – though of course God's grace makes us capable of establishing something of his kingdom in our world as well.

These paragraphs are purposely skating round the question of original sin. There is an imbalance in the traditional doctrine. We inherit the sin of the world, no doubt about it; but we also inherit the history of grace, the story of human fidelity to the self-communication of God. Maybe we have an inclination to evil, and Paul at places picks up the biblical and rabbinical doctrine of this 'slant'; but we also have an inclination to good, because God's grace gets in first. Catholic theology resists going on and on about sin, and tries to hold the two in balance.

There should be no sense of guilt about sin, because it is forgiven. We can *celebrate* our forgiveness at the beginning of mass. Not only is God compassionate towards our frailty, our growth pangs, because he has made us that way; but his grace is a force which heals and effectively overcomes both sin and sins. That is forgiveness as a reality, and not just as a sort of mental discounting on the part of God.

Sin is profoundly important, though not a matter for guilt, and a sense of sin is crucial for Christian life. Jesus's saying, 'I have not come to call the just, but sinners to repentance', can be understood as meaning that those who are complacent, closed, self-righteous, are impervious to God's call to grow into the likeness of his Son; only those who know their need and sickness will be open to the transforming power of his healing Spirit. There must be conversion, a turning of the heart to God.

Sins, at least in those who are sincerely trying to serve God, are trivial, repetitive and boring: the regular laundry list we present to God, asking for his forgiveness and help. They are more a symptom than a cause of disorder, though they would reinforce the degree to which we share in sin if they were unacknowledged, if they were simply accepted without resistance as part of being human.

8. Theology today is variously seeking to overcome, or to get beneath, the idea that our moral life is a series of disparate acts, which can be separately weighed by ourselves or by anyone else (a confessor). They are searching for the unity of the person which underlies the acts, and for the person-to-person relationship with God that is going on. Our friendship with God and share in his life cannot be totally lost by sudden particular acts (mortal sins), any more than it can be totally gained by single conscious acts.

Rahner, Schoonenberg, Fuchs, Häring and others explore the central and unified commitment of the person that underlies particular choices.[3] They write of basic freedom, basic moral acts, fundamental option, transcendental freedom; of the underlying commitment by which we progressively determine ourselves as persons. As with knowledge, so with freedom: human beings have a capacity to know or to opt for historical persons and realities, because they have a capacity to know and opt for God. So, God is present in every free act as its horizon, as its fundamental impulse and final goal. Not every free act achieves the same depth and thoroughness of self-commitment, but in their free acts humans are always realizing or constituting themselves in response to

[3]Karl Rahner, *Grace in Freedom*, Search Press 1969; P. Schoonenberg, *Man and Sin*, Sheed and Ward 1965; J. Fuchs, *Human Values and Christian Morality*, Gill and Macmillan 1970; B. Häring, *Sin in the Secular Age*, St Paul Publications 1974, and *Free and Faithful in Christ*, Vol. 1, St Paul Publications 1978.

God, in loving acceptance or in rejection.

The close analyses found in such writers rely partly on the findings of psychology, partly on understandings of personality and freedom that owe much to the philosophies of Kant and Heidegger. Their analyses do not make easy reading, and do not always carry conviction as true to experience. If one has understood, they chiefly seem to be saying two things. The first is that our relationship to God is a cumulative life-story, a love story, which develops underlying attitudes, emphases, concerns, which our daily living can only by degrees set firmly in one direction or the other. The second is that only in the transition from life to death could our option be totally for or against God, because only in eternity do we wholly encounter him.

9. The word 'alienation' is used widely, one might even say bandied about, in some modern treatments of sin. But one may search in vain for any coherent meaning of the term. Pre-cartesian man saw himself as alienated, estranged, from God by his sinful condition. The more he deviated from the goal given him by God, together with its laws of conduct, the more he disintegrated internally and became estranged from his true self, and the more havoc he wreaked in society. But the philosophy of subjectivity that has developed since Descartes now presents us with the opposite contention: man's future lies solely in his own hands; he becomes estranged from his true self if he accepts dependence on any other; his greatness lies in his inner freedom and in his responsibility for himself and his world; belief in God or in any assured salvation is the extreme and abject abdication of personal responsibility and of the roots of selfhood.

Perhaps the achilles heel of this pervasive climate of philosophical atheism is that it ignores a human being's first experience, that of being loved, and the need everyone has of being loved in order to grow into an integrated person capable of giving the self in love and trust. The gospel of salvation then becomes: in this is love, not that we have the resources and the hope of constructing a loving society from the recesses of our freedom, but that God first loved us and gives his love as a free gift to be accepted.

However that may be, we cannot speak convincingly of sin

unless we can speak convincingly of salvation, and thus determine the nature of sin and sins as all that opposes it. Otherwise our discourse and our liturgical celebrations will alienate people, at least in the sense of turning them off. We need to show how faith in the salvation offered us in Christ gives meaning to our lives, and therefore to ourselves; how it gives meaning to our tragedies, losses, frustrations and deprivations; how it creates respect and love for other persons and enables us to create a more human world; how it gives hope.

These reflections on sin originated in a contribution to a symposium on the *Spiritual Exercises* of Ignatius of Loyola. And so they end, by way of contrast, with a few, and partial, insights into the sixteenth-century theology of sin with which Ignatius operated and which perhaps has seeped into our own first understanding of the matter. I was asked to consider whether a retreat director today could simply present the text of Ignatius as it stands. In what he called the 'First Week' of his Exercises, Ignatius confronts the person making a retreat with what he considered to be the basics of Christian life – the purpose of our creation and the need to 'save our souls'.

10. We need first of all to recall and face up to certain features of the first four Exercises on sin.

(*a*) The soul is a prisoner in the body: the whole self is condemned to live in exile among beasts (Exx 47). To help me see the ugliness and deformity of sin, I should consider the foulness and ugliness of my body and see myself as an ulcerous sore (Exx 58).

(*b*) Many have been lost for a single sin, or for fewer sins than mine (Exx 48, 52). Eternal condemnation is a just retribution for one sinful act against infinite goodness (52). I should see myself as a sinner led in chains before the Judge (74).

(*c*) These exercises are intended to produce a sense of shame (48, 74), self-loathing (50), disgust (63), as well as perfect sorrow and intense grief (55).

Even apart from the somewhat lurid details, the soul-body dichotomy, which entered deep into Christian spirituality, is not compatible with our understanding of the incarnation, the redemption of the world, the *milieu divin*, the building of the kingdom on earth.

> Though made of body and soul, man is one. Through his bodily composition he gathers to himself the elements of the material world. Thus they reach their crown through him, and through him raise their voice in free praise of the Creator. For this reason man is not allowed to despise his bodily life. Rather, he is obliged to regard his body as good and honourable since God has created it and will raise it up on the last day. . . .[4]

Next, we would be very chary of instilling 'alienating' images of God. And we must note that concern for improving the quality of human life is absent. The thought is of the salvation and damnation of individuals. The spirituality is other-worldly.

Ignatius may principally have intended the Exercises to convert worldly clerics into zealous apostles: hence the colloquy before the cross of Christ (52). But there can surely be no doubt that he meant these Exercises to be done by people of spiritual quality, anxious to serve God better, and not only by rumbustious sinners. For our part, we would be very chary of encouraging self-loathing. Many will come in need of encouragement and hope rather than of puncturing, in need of finding greater meaning in their faith for coping with life.

On the other hand, a sense of sin has virtually disappeared from our secular society. And sorrow for sin must remain an integral part of Christian awareness and spirituality. So a way must be found to treat sin so that sorrow is a dimension of faith, hope and love.

11. No, we cannot give the text as it stands. That would be sheer fundamentalism. One way ahead would be to argue that Ignatius's text is 'Spiritual Exercises', not '*The* Spiritual Exercises'. His first paragraph suggests that there could be any number of appropriate spiritual exercises other than those he offers in his little book, and the director might be free to put the retreatant through any exercises suited to his needs. On the other hand, the Exercises have a basic structure and aim at

[4]*Gaudium et Spes*, n. 14.

specific goals. If we have understood these, we should feel confident about working out our own exercises in terms of modern insights and needs, to reach the same goals.

Another way might be to highlight the contrasts between sixteenth and twentieth-century understandings of sin, to help retreatants to reach their own perceptions, the object of a retreat being to find God, not to work out the perfect theology.

12. One qualification suggests itself. Contemporary theology speaks much of the place that stories have in any religion. Stories are in, myths are out ('myth' being the Greek for 'story')![5] One can hardly over-estimate the influence of the Exodus story in shaping the Jewish attitude to God and to life. Much of the Bible is narrative. Most people communicate with each other in narrative, rather than in abstractions. Stories encapsulate one's vision of life and its meanings.

Let us tell the stories of the fall of the angels, and the fall of Adam and Eve, precisely as stories and not as dogma. The point is not whether they happened, but the meanings, the vision that they convey.

The fall of the angels is the story of enclosure in self carried to its absolute. We can substitute 'I will not love' for 'I will not serve' without lessening the majesty of God, who is more majestic in loving than in giving commands. The angels put self in place of God, whom we have learned to know as the God who loves unconditionally.

The fall of Adam and Eve is the story of the misuse of creatures. They put creatures in place of God, which is idolatry. They did not put bad things in place of God, but small things like independence, esteem, success (furniture, colour television . . .). They went out of paradise in coarse garments, showing the degradation of the image of God in which they had been created. If we can take Teilhard's point about the alpha and the omega, the Genesis story is not about a primal innocence man ever possessed, but about what man and woman are called by God to become.

13. The chief thrust of these observations is that you cannot understand sin in itself. It is the obverse of a gospel. In Ignatius's day everyone assumed the gospel as it was then

[5]See J. Taylor (ed.), *Believing in the Church*, SPCK 1981, Ch. 4.

articulated in the characteristically Basque and Catalonian
colours of salvation and damnation. So you could portray sin
vividly in terms of millions cascading into hell. Pure El Greco,
one might say. Today we must preach the gospel in a world
that has ceased to hear it, but a credible gospel in a threatened
world. We do not have to paint imaginative pictures to
produce grief, sorrow, inadequacy, futility, degradation. The
media din them into our eyes and ears every day. There are
50,000 nuclear weapons around. There have been 150
'conventional' wars since World War II. Élitist opulence is
surrounded by mass starvation. There are precious few
countries in the world where the ordinary freedoms are
enjoyed. The problem is not how to portray sin, but how to
portray salvation.

One of the Pauline theologies of salvation is in terms of
reconciliation, and the church now uses the term for the
sacrament of penance. 'God was in Christ', we quote,
'reconciling the world to himself' – and so reconciling men to
one another. If we can make that bite, if we can translate it into
the realities of what mankind might do, and what we might do
in our little areas of life, then perhaps we can bring home to
ourselves and to others what it is to preach Jesus Christ today,
and what it is to reject him.

9

THE MYSTERY OF GOOD AND EVIL

Suffering

The problem of evil is a problem of *human* suffering. Clearly we condemn and try to eliminate cruelty to animals, that is, human cruelty to animals. But there is nothing we can do about the cruelty of animals to each other. And we are not disturbed by, or resentful at, animals dying from natural disaster such as flood or fire or drought. Nor is it 'a problem' that some animals feed on other animals. Life feeds on life. That is the way things are, the way the world is, the nature of life, and we cannot even imagine another sort of world. It is human suffering that is the problem.

And it is a religious problem. Or, as long as it is a problem, it is a religious one. We feel resentful against God that human beings suffer so much: there is religious poetry, as in the Psalms, in which men rail against God. Or we declare that God cannot be good to create such a world, or to look on and do nothing about it. Having got that far, our minds are forced to conclude that, if God is not good, he does not exist. At this point our minds should go on to conclude that, if there is no God, there is no problem: there is just suffering, as brute fact, and try as we may we cannot prevent or alleviate most of it; we can only scratch the surface or stave it off. But it is *not* just an intellectual problem reaching a cold and callous 'solution'. It is a strongly emotional problem. And if we deny that there can be a God behind all this, we are still left with the strong resentment – against life.

Because it is both an intellectual and a strongly emotional or religious problem, attempts to tackle it or answer the question of God's goodness and omnipotence on the one side, and human suffering on the other, must operate at both levels – the intellectual, and that of religious feeling or sensitivity or intuition or perception or sense of mystery. Answers at the intellectual level will not seem to be answers, because the emotional resentment is not touched by them. The problem does not arise at the intellectual but at the emotional level. But it does pose serious theoretical questions which have to be faced.

The theoretical level

When one thinks about it, the problem divides into two: that of human suffering caused by human beings themselves; and the suffering arising from sickness of mind and body and from natural disasters.

Before we look at each, however, there is one level of generally 'resentful question' which embraces both. Why did God not create a perfect world in which there was no evil from either source? The questioner is asking for the impossible. For 'to be created' entails 'to be imperfect', and so 'a perfect created world' is a contradiction in terms. Only God is perfect and has or is the fullness of being. To be created is to have limited being and perfection: so God could not create a world where there was perfect goodness, perfect harmony, etc. It is not a limitation on his omnipotence, but in the possible created material. It is not a limitation on God's omnipotence not to be able to create the contradictory, the cubic sphere, etc. Whatever created being exists, has its limited being, cube or sphere, not both. A man is not a woman. Man or woman is placid or excitable, not both. To be anything or anyone is to have specific constituents or ingredients and not others, and to have certain qualities to a limited extent: a 'perfectly intelligent' man is not possible and is unimaginable. That which exists is limited by precisely the being that it has.

Very well, then, the questioner might come back: but why is there *so much* suffering in the world? God could surely have created a world which, even if not perfect, was far less imperfect than this one either in moral evil or in sickness and natural disaster. Well, that will have to be looked at from many sides in the course of the ensuing reflections. But there is an immediate point to consider. Life grows from the small to the great, from the immature, inexperienced and ill-equipped towards the mature and wise. The more that instinct prevails in a living being, the quicker it reaches maturity – and a set limit of development and performance. The more that intelligence dominates, the slower the growth and the less are there any limits to future development, either in the individual or in the species throughout its history. So is the questioner perhaps smuggling in a non-question? There is only this world for us to argue about and to try to make sense of: this world which we have learned to understand in terms of growth and development, and not as some machine of intricate but fixed interrelated parts which would function timelessly the same. And in a world such as this one, from the nature of the case, human knowledge will grow, human control will grow; the reality humans consider will itself develop; and so at earlier stages of their own short lives or in the life of the species human beings will be less equipped and more defenceless, less able to prevent or cure suffering, than at later stages – except that in some of their developments they bring new sorts of suffering on themselves. It is meaningless to ask why God did not create some totally other and unimaginable world. The only meaningful task is to try to understand this one.

We have already begun an answer to the problem of the quantity and quality of suffering from sickness and from natural disaster in a world created by a God supposedly both good and omnipotent. It is the result of human ignorance. If we knew everything, knew all there was to know (perfect intelligence once more), sickness would be prevented, children would not be bred with congenital defects of mind or body (indeed, would we not all have standard 'perfect equipment'?); floods, earthquakes and droughts would be foreseen long in advance and their ill effects avoided if they could not themselves be prevented, etc. If we knew everything! Can you begin to imagine human life in which everything knowable was already known? No possibility of discovery, of newness, of surprise, of initiative, of search, of curiosity, of inventive-

ness, of growth, of being somebody who had not already been
turned off the production belt time without number. . . . Life
would have ground to a halt. It would have cancelled itself out.
It would have ceased to be human. So, the meaning of life lies
in endeavour, to stretch out beyond the good to the better, to
transcend itself. But that is something to be picked up in
another context.

In the previous chapter on theologies of sin, some of the
considerations were briefly sketched which help us to understand how it can be that there is so much deliberate moral evil,
causing so much human suffering, in a world created by a God
who is good. There is, first, the inevitable tragedy of our
identifying ourselves (discovering and becoming who we are)
by identifying ourselves *against* other groups, and in our only
slowly learning that our own fulfilment is wholly bound up
with the fulfilment of others, ultimately of all others; and the
fact that this is true of the race as a whole and yet that each new
individual has to learn not to make the same mistakes all over
again which he will only do if this is the lesson taught by the
society into which he is born. Then, there are all the
implications of understanding the world in Teilhardian
fashion as a growing whole, created by God to be transformed
(matter and spirit together) into the kingdom of his Son: in
such a view the necessary implications of development from
the less perfect to the more perfect stand out clearly; and one
glimpses the truth that salvation (like sin) cannot be simply an
individualistic affair but, seen as far as we can see it from
God's end, must be the salvation of the whole (which perhaps
does not necessarily imply the salvation of each individual);
that the meaning of history (of life as man experiences it) can
only be grasped at the end of history; that somehow in God's
plan the damaged, truncated, deformed lives will be 'made
whole'; that we are where we are, for better or for worse, for
sin or for salvation, because of the generations who have
preceded us; and that we leave the world better or worse than
we found it for our children and for their generations to come.

There is one consideration touched on in the last chapter
which is central to the problem of evil and needs to be fully
explored. Man is made for God. Whether he knows it or not,
the deepest and ultimately explanatory driving force of his

being is that he is searching for God, yearning for God, voyaging towards God. Man can know from the experience of life that he is a restless being, a discontented being, that his reach always stretches out beyond his grasp, that he can never settle to a pattern of life from birth to death as we imagine the animals to do, but will always be out beyond himself, discovering, striving for the greater wisdom, beauty, fullness of life, happiness. Aquinas held that man could not know that God had made him for himself, that it was God for whom he was all the time searching, unless God told him so, revealed this truth (or rather revealed himself) to him. He could not know without revelation that it was a divine discontent that drove him. Man is made, not to 'possess' God as some sort of object, nor even (*pace* Aquinas and his aristotelianism) to know God in a merely contemplative or intellectual sense: he is made already sharing the life of God and destined to share it fully. The force that drives him is already the approach of God, the birth and struggling within him of God's life, the Spirit of God. (This could not be grasped in the context of a theological model that added grace, the supernatural, to a timeless essence or nature; it can only be grasped, or defended, within a growth model which sees the 'order of grace' as the only one that has ever existed and the supernatural context or horizon of man's existence and experience as what constitutes him as specifically human.)

The mystery and problem of evil as it is usually posed is a one-sided affair. We never, or rarely, set it against the mystery of good. Heaven we do not regard as a problem; it is hell which we cannot assimilate. Happiness, however bursting, is no problem, only suffering. Happiness and fulfilment are somehow regarded as our due, even if their content remains elusive; and this is perhaps one indication of an underlying awareness that we are made for God. But it is precisely and only a being who can hope as man hopes, that can despair as man despairs; only a being who can love with the intensity with which man can love, that can also hate with the depths and violence of man's hate; only one who can experience the deep or wild ecstasy of human joys, that can suffer as only man can suffer, not just physically but mentally and through and through. The loss of a child is something a mother will never wholly get over, because there is something undying in a mother's love for her child. It is the *same* human sensitivity, spirituality, that accounts for man's heights and for his depths; his limitless creativity, his abysmal destructiveness; his artistic perfection, his barbaric cruelty. *Corruptio optimi pessima.* In his heights and in his depths man somehow touches on the divine and the diabolic: he is only capable of one because he is capable of the other. Angels and devils are symbols of the extreme edges of man's own experience.

So, it is the *same* driving force, *élan vital*, of God's summoning and empowering Spirit that makes man capable, here and now in his this-worldly existence, of these heights and depths. It is because it is the summons of God that is at work that such an uncontrollably powerful force permeates human life. It is comparatively easy to recognize the power of God at work in heroic lives of courage, endurance, expansiveness, self-sacrificing love: let us say in a Mother Teresa. Dare we also say the opposite? In Thomas Kineally's book, *Schindler's Ark*, the camp commandant is portrayed in such horrifying terms of sodden, callous, bestial brutality, as he blows out the brains of a young woman doctor to show who is in charge of the outfit, or herds Jewish children into baking cattle-trucks to despatch them to the gas chamber. Can we have the courage to recognize that no human being could be so diabolical unless he were charged with the power of God? Can we even have the courage to say that, deep at the roots of his being, it was the driving-force of God's life, indeed love, that enabled Anton to be the consummate beast that he was? And can we perhaps pause to wonder, given the limitations of his personal ability, and the conditioning process which he breathed and swam in, whether we can judge him? Finally, can we even dare to wonder whether, at the roots of his egotism and his hates, which make him a god to himself, he was aware of the life-force of God beating through him?

And so we are forced to a stark theological conclusion. It is God who is ultimately responsible for the good and the evil in human experience, even in the moral sphere. For God made man for himself and thereby implanted in him a force capable of producing heaven – and hell. At any rate, heaven and hell in our experience, for hell as a reality, as a final state of man has problems of its own (it is hard to see how becoming totally a non-person differs from ceasing to be). It is God who is ultimately responsible. How could he be God for us, if he were not ultimately responsible? And those who reject the idea of God because of the evil that persists in life are at least allowing 'God' to be God. There is something mildly impertinent, in a well-meaning way, in the whole enterprise of theodicy, of justifying the ways of God to man. Is it God who needs justifying – or our bitterness and resentments? Is it not mere tinkering to talk of God 'permitting' moral and physical evil for the sake of man's growth and man's freedom, while somehow keeping himself aloof, uninvolved? If he created the small creature, destined and called to grow, he created the possibility of human suffering through ignorance. If he created the free will that could stand over against him, he created not just the possibility but the inevitability of sin and sins (theologians simply must come clean on that point): he did so in creating the possibility of grace. The weakness of theodicy is that it tries to tackle the problem of evil within the confines of a doctrine of creation, and without the dimension of grace within which in fact evil, like good, exists; in which in fact man exists.

It is hopelessly one-sided to be burdened and broken down with a sense of human suffering and to take for granted to the point of insensitivity the overwhelming richness and beauty of life, of the marvels of nature, of the creative genius of humanity – in short, of persons. Every human development, from the wheel to the silicone chip and beyond, is double-handed, bringing new opportunities, new enrichment of life, and new problems and perils. People are crushed beneath wheels. Television and the rest of our communications systems unite the human family in awareness and concern, they often bring untold benefits to the sick and the lonely, they create the possibility of a new one-world world; and also without any question they charge the football crowd and the unemployed disadvantaged black youth with a 'world' force of excitement and involvement; they give to the terrorist the publicity he needs for his cause, they endanger the values and standards of society, etc. It is no good blaming the media. They batter us with disasters on the front pages and in the news bulletins, but are full of the good news of the building of the kingdom throughout the spread of their pages and their programmes. The media have their problem of making news rather than reporting it (hounding a cabinet minister to resignation, or giving terrorism and hooliganism its publicity value, for example), but that is just one more instance of the ambivalence of human achievement, which brings with its advantages new problems for the human race to solve.

So, if we can recognize the loving-kindness of God our Saviour in the joys of life, in the intimacy and fulfilment of human love, in marriage, in parenthood, in friendship, in the intricate delicacy and variety of colour and sound and texture in natural life, and in the infinitely varied satisfactions of human achievement – in short, in persons; if we can simply 'be', and see and hear and feel the God of love coming at us from every quarter with the gift of life; then, can we not also open ourselves to the majesty of God who is no comfortable and domesticated correlative to our here and now bourgeois suburban and parochial horizons of well-being but God – the explosive, creative, commanding and destructive force of absolute life? There is much that is theoretically problematic, and indeed unacceptable, in the Psalmist's picture of the God of wrath and judgment who castigates the infidelities of his beloved and chosen people; just as there is much that is theoretically problematic about the worshipper who rails resentfully at the deafness and blindness of God to the injustices of life. But at least here is a God who is God, before whom it is we who need justifying, not he. And if we can see that God is always the source and origin and beginning, and is always first and has the initiative; and if we can see and feel that he is steadfast in love and merciful and infinitely forgiving; then can we not also glimpse the truth that, being, God, he is a devouring fire?

The level of religious symbols

We have already gone some way into the 'answer' to the mystery of evil in terms of religious symbolism. You do not 'speak to' the young wife whose husband has died of cancer, or been killed in some senseless road accident, in coldly theoretical terms. You do not comfort her with the intellectual truth that God could not have created a perfect world. You have to relate to such suffering in terms of flesh and blood and feeling, powerful imagery and poetic symbol.

God did not answer the problem of evil by intellectual discourse. The 'wisdom' books of the Old Testament chip away at the mystery, but do not get anywhere except as a witness to man tortured by the mystery of good and evil. Job is silenced, not by answers but by the majesty of God.

God answered the problem by action, by a living response. Being God, he cannot deploy himself without remainder into human terms that we can wholly grasp, so that we can then fit together all the pieces of the puzzle to our satisfaction – and reduce him to our level and dimensions. Being God he remains the mystery of ultimate being and life.

Being God, he is ultimately responsible. And therefore he *cares*, cares in a divine way. So he translated himself and his loving and caring into human and historical terms – not human terms which disclosed his reality and his relationship to us in wholly packaged and assimilable fashion, but terms of immanence in which his transcendence could be encountered and related to. The wisdom, the plan, the outgoing self-gift of God was made flesh and dwelt amongst us. Not just 'made man' in some general or abstract sense, such as taking the essential 'parts' which constitute a human being; but made 'flesh', entering into and involving himself permanently in the conditions of our human experience, conditions of frailty, mortality, sensitivity, vulnerability, insecurity, failure. Abject failure. The teaching and the miracles of Jesus show at all points the love of God at work in human life to bring tenderness and love and healing, to set free the oppressed and those paralysed by religious and other inhibitions, to conquer all the forces which attack and threaten and wound the body and the spirit. And yet, he was to all appearances overcome by the rigidities and narrow zeal of virtuous men, he was rejected, he was put out of the way as a threat to good order and stability, even by death on a cross. The cross of Jesus shows irrevocably that, because God is responsible, God cares about human suffering, God enters it, shares it, triumphs through it. I speak of religious 'symbols' because the life and the death and the resurrection of Jesus cannot be turned into cause-and-effect mechanisms within the compass of our human (Western) understanding and intellectual control. They are not just symbols in the sense of evocative images; they are events of time and eternity which involve us to the depths of our personal being and responses, and so can only be grasped and expressed emotionally, evocatively, poetically. They are events which are gateways to the unfathomable mystery of God. We speak of redemption, atonement, expiation (in scripture the word means 'cleansing'), reconciliation, justification, salvation, liberation, eternal life, resurrection, exaltation, glorification, fulfilment, consummation. These terms are not 'explanations', not descriptions of wholly intelligible processes, but very partial attempts to find images and words for what we encounter in the mystery of Christ: for we encounter God, and not explanatory processes. And it is not words that you put before suffering humanity, shocked by the encounter with evil, but the tangible reality of God's caring, God's total involvement in the remotest depths and corners of human sensitivity and experience, in Jesus Christ.

Should it surprise us that the love story of God's self-gift to man is both sublime and excruciating? Is not that just what love is for us? And if we are to tangle with God, what then? Theory and 'answers' give way at this point to the experience of the mystics.

10

THE DESIGN OF GOD

A basic and pervasive conviction of the Old Testament is that God is Lord of history, that he guides or steers or governs the course of events; nature is the instrument of his blessings and his judgments on men. Indeed, it was through this conviction that Israel moved from its earlier 'henotheism' (Yahweh is the one and only God of Israel) to strict monotheism (Yahweh is the only God there is, and he manages all history for the sake of his elect). Israel interpreted its own past history in this light: they were victorious in battle because God was on their side, defeated because of their infidelities; carried off into exile because of the 'adultery' of their kings in turning away from Yahweh to false gods, brought back from exile because of God's mercy using the pagan king Cyrus for his purposes. It is to be noted that this notion of the design of God as Lord of history is in collective or communal terms: the plan is for the people as a whole and for the destiny to which God leads them; it is not concerned with the fortunes of individuals. The fact that the innocent often suffer while the wicked prosper was much puzzled over in the wisdom literature and notably in the Book of Job, but without any very convincing answer emerging. It all ends up in mystery: God's thoughts are not our thoughts.

Both the belief in God's design for Israel as Lord of history, and perplexities about the lot of individuals, suggest a picture of God managing events, intervening to change the course of events, for purposes of his own which may well not be clear at the time, and possibly not later. And it is remarkable that Christian writers and preachers have often themselves tried to fathom the question of God's providence, or purposes in history, with the same ideas of steering, managing or intervening. Such ideas give rise to obvious problems about God's omnipotence and man's free will: is man's freedom only illusory, with God's greater power somehow steering things the way he wants them to go? Or should we say simply that God's action is 'transcendent', of a higher order, not to be set in competition with or on the same level as man's action, and that it is just a mystery how he attains his purposes through our free actions, so that we can only trust that he will? Trust, for instance, that he loves and has a care for humanity and will not allow us to destroy ourselves with nuclear weapons? And, at the level of the individual, people sometimes puzzle over the question 'what God is up to', what his purposes are when certain things happen to me, what design he may have for my future, how I am to discover his undisclosed will and carry it out, etc. Surely my life will be a failure if I have not carried out God's will for me, if I have unknowingly taken wrong turnings and not matched up to his plan. There is or used to be the neurotic idea of the 'spoiled vocation', which seems to suggest that if I have not found and followed my true calling, then God cannot be expected to be pleased with or have much interest in anything else I may do in life.

It is remarkable that Christians still sometimes think this way (though they tend to ask what God is up to only when bad or unhappy things come their way and not when good ones do). It is remarkable, because the New Testament has changed all that. As Paul repeatedly says, the secret is out, there is no secret any more. God only ever had one plan for man. Christ. Christ and his kingdom. The transformation of the world into the kingdom of Christ. Israel's developing understandings of God's design were only preliminaries and aspirations, which reached their realization and fulfilment in Jesus Christ. He *is* the fulfilment of God's promise. In him there is a new and eternal covenant, one not to be supplanted by any other. Not just for Israel. Not just for possession of the land. Not for an anointed king to rule over them who would make all nations subject to them. But a covenant of love with men, to transform them into a holy people living in justice and peace, with all the enemies that threaten humanness overcome.

The grace of Christ is a force that stirs and works at the heart of every man and woman to transform their lives. It is God's gift of himself, addressing us, summoning us, challenging us, to give ourselves in response and grow into the stature of the new man, Christ. This force *is* God's care and providence for us. It *is* his control of history. It works through *us*. We do not need to look for any other.

Will this force prevail in human history? Will men grow in mutual respect and love, in peace and justice, or will greed, ambition and antagonisms prevail and the nuclear bomb settle the issue once and for all? As was briefly mentioned in the chapter on the theology of sin, there is no great guarantee from inside history, from the human track record, that things will come out right, that the human race will take the right turnings. One could argue that mankind has shown a remarkable capacity for survival and for overcoming the problems that have been created by all its advances. But that is a precarious argument, because we have got to the point where there is no longer room for any mistakes. If you look at it simply from the point of view of human wisdom and powers, you could hardly give the human race more than a fifty-fifty chance. And that is where the hope component of Christian faith comes in, the element it drew from Jewish faith of which it sees itself as the new fullness. Human victory is a dicey affair. But Christ's victory is not, it does not hang in the balance of the future. It has already been won. He has died, he *is* risen, he *will* come. He is the one who comes. He will come, not at some apocalyptic point in the future when the heavens clash in cosmic battle, but progressively all the time. He will build his kingdom steadily through us. He has been doing it throughout the history of humanity. It is for all of us to build that kingdom around us wherever we can in the small circuit of our own lives.

Which brings us down to the lot of the individual and the design of God for each of us in our own lives. Paul really said it all in Romans 8.28. He did not say, 'All things work together unto good'. He was not propounding a theory or theology of providence that encouraged us to shut our eyes and believe that, however ghastly the disasters that befell us and those we love, however horrifying and terrifying 'the news' of the wars robberies rapes muggings floods famines ... God is manipulating events to some mysterious good purpose of his own which might become clear if and when we get to heaven. He said: 'To those who love God, all things work together unto good.' That is to say, God is not picking this or that event to happen to me; but, in all events that happen to me, good or bad, I can encounter and find God, I can grow in his love, I can receive his gift of himself, I can receive his transforming power and mediate it to others, I can build his kingdom. It is the lesson and pattern of Jesus' own life.

Thomas Aquinas treated the question of God's providence very fully in Part I of his *Summa Theologiae* (qq. 19–23), and set up a most important theoretical model for understanding and speaking of God's will. We go astray, he says, if we think of God first willing the end (his ultimate design) and then, and because of that, willing this, that or the other means. We should think of God as having only a single act of will, a single plan: he does not will the means by a separate act because he wills the end; he wills that these means should be means to that end. He does not intervene in natural or human causality but establishes a single order, the supernatural or Christ-order: he wills that whatever results from natural and human causality should be means for me to grow in eternal life.

In Matthew's gospel Jesus is constantly saying, 'Do not be anxious!'. Anxieties about God's will for me are a hangover from pre-Christian attempts to fathom God as Lord of history, and sometimes a hangover from fatalist or predestinarian views of God's design for the world. I should not be ridden with questions about what God means, or intends, or is planning, by the ups and downs of life; or imagine him as having some special blueprint for me which is mysterious and secret which I may be failing to match up to, while God shakes his head over my missing out on his plan. His plan is only and always to give himself to me in all the events of life, in joy and in sorrow, in success and in failure, in life and in death. Because, for all the other ups and downs of life, it will ultimately be in death. When he knew that he was suffering from cancer and had only some few months to live, Bishop John Robinson wrote a circular letter to a wide group of friends on finding God in cancer. This is the true discipleship of

Jesus, whose successes were soon overcome by failure, whose open offer of God's salvation to all men, for free, so shook and threatened the establishments of this world that they put him out of the way. He found God in the lilies of the field; he found God in the love of his mother and of disciples and friends; he found God in the halt, the blind, the leper, the marginalized, the oppressor and the oppressed; he found him in the solitude of prayer; he found him in rejection, betrayal, the howling mob, the torture of the cross. In this sign we conquer.

Out of all the theological flurry of centuries about election and predestination, only one theological question remains for our understanding: that of God's omnipotence and man's free will.

It is not a problem about God giving or not giving 'the same grace' to all men. Grace is not an object, a thing issued from the heavenly cupboard, least of all a standard issue. It is a personal relationship. And because it is personal it is different for each: there are no two persons the same. God does offer himself to all, as a saving and sharing God, where and who we are in history. And certainly in the unfolding of his plan he chooses or elects men and women to particular roles. He chose Israel and the prophets. He chose Mary for a quite unique role, and it is God's choice and her role in his saving plan through her human and physical motherhood which sets her apart in Christian devotion, rather than any interior qualities of her spirituality. He chose Peter, James and John. He chooses believing Christians today, as he has done in all ages, to fulfil specially prominent and effective roles in building the kingdom – Benedict, Francis, Dominic, Ignatius. He chooses us all for our own role or vocation.

Nor is it a time problem. The 'pre' could be dropped from the word 'predestination', if it needs to be used at all. Then all that is left is God's choice, election. It is not a matter of choosing some and not others. He chooses all. The point is that the spontaneous and creative giving originates from him.

It is not a problem about election or destination to the church of some and not others, since the church is not the sole or even the ordinary means of salvation: it is the sign, the embodied witness in history, of what God does for all in Christ.

It is not a problem about whether God wishes all men to be saved (he does), or whether he gives to all 'sufficient grace'. He gives himself (not measured quantities of a thing called 'grace') to each, and what he asks of each by way of response is something he has not told us. What is clear is the responsibility of those to whom he has given 'grace upon grace'.

So all that is left is the question of God's omnipotence and man's free will. And that is only a problem or an impasse if the question is wrongly set up as an apparent conflict between human freedom of choice and God's superior or managerial powers. The question is already answered if one accepts that the *only* way in which God steers history is that of giving himself as the transcendent mystery of absolute life at the root and heart of all human experience. This and this alone is the exercise of his omnipotence. God is always creator. His gift of himself to me makes me to be me. His gift creates my freedom: the instant pressure of his loving self-offering liberates me progressively from the smallness and limitations of my origins and horizons, and draws me ever onwards into self-surpassing transcendence, into greater personhood, greater freedom, greater responsible determination of my life and self-hood. Augustine, who thought in terms of moral psychology and not of an abstract mechanics of grace and nature, wrote eloquently about God's grace as healing and liberating.

The collect of the Tenth Sunday after Pentecost (now moved on and imaginatively renamed the Twenty-sixth Sunday in Ordinary Time) says it all:

Father, you show your almighty power in your mercy and forgiveness.
Continue to fill us with your gifts of love.
Help us to hurry towards the eternal life you promise and come to share
   in the joys of your kingdom.

And as the Latin says it so magnificently, let us have that too:

Deus, qui omnipotentiam tuam parcendo maxime et miserando manifestas: multiplica super nos misericordiam tuam; ut, ad tua promissa currentes, caelestium bonorum facias esse consortes. Per Dominum.

II

PRAYING

(I can almost hear God saying 'You've got a neck, writing on prayer!' But this is the chapter that makes sense of all the rest and knits them together. Maybe it should have come at the beginning.)

Intercessory prayer

We don't really believe in a God who intervenes, who keeps interrupting ordinary processes of cause and effect by slipping in little actions of his own and diverting the course of events. So why do we go in for so many prayers of intercession, from our earliest days in our private prayers (like Christopher Robin's 'God bless mummy, I know that's right – wasn't it fun in the bath tonight!') and in the church's liturgy? What do we think we are doing? What effect do we think it has? The question worries a lot of people who nevertheless would feel greatly deprived if they could not pray in this way for others.

Well, first of all it affects us. That is by no means a whole answer, as the ostensible purpose of intercessory prayer is to change things for the better for other people; but it is not unimportant, and it is a necessary foundation for the rest of the answer. I am not thinking of what must be called frivolous prayers (for a fine day for the church fête, or that our side should win): we can only consider prayers as true prayers and as problematic, if they are concerned with the kingdom, and that certainly includes healing and averting the ills that assail men and women, or more positively bringing the goodies of the kingdom into people's lives. Serious prayer affects us. Serious prayers arise out of and deepen a real concern for others. They put me in tune with the starving, or the hates and fears people experience, or their pain and distress, or the heroic endurance of the persecuted and of prisoners of conscience. They are serious if they are about something serious and if I am serious about them – not if I rattle off some set list of intercessions, the urbanity and formality of which almost prevents my being involved. Serious prayers affect me. And that does two things. First of all it challenges me to do something about it and so I become vulnerable in praying, I take a certain risk and responsibility: to visit the sick, to co-operate with Amnesty, Oxfam etc., to drop a line, to be involved. In other words, to give myself in some way. We must build the kingdom in the small circuit of our own lives, and prayers of intercession involve me more in that. How the world would be changed if everybody did that!

Secondly, and this is where we move on into a more difficult area, sensitizing and involving myself tunes me in or plugs me in to a more pervasive spiritual concern or concern of the spirit. I am charged by and add my charge to a common spiritual force. I am spelling spirit with a small 's' at this point and I am pointing to an only partly explored area, the spiritual energy or life-force that is shared by human beings. At risk of being laughed at, I will start at a lower level. Good farmers are 'kind to the soil'. All who knew my mother said she had green fingers. She had a feeling for things growing in a garden. She talked to them, sometimes praising and admiring, sometimes encouraging, sometimes openly abusing them. And we all establish rapport with dogs, cats, horses. . . . Dogs certainly like being included in the conversation and are sensitive to being part of the family. I do believe in communication of life with life, some sort of mutual influence, even at the lower levels. With people it is more obvious. When someone is distressed, you need to listen, to receive, to feel with them, to be space into which they can enter freely; you need to share, absorb, mop up their distress; you need to let them explode, or mourn, or resent, to someone receptive, not to an unhearing and unfeeling void. They don't want you to argue with them, straighten them out, reshape their attitudes, or offer any sort of resistance. They want you to share their feelings. And that sharing is very significant and healing for them. It helps them to cope with themselves and with whatever circumstances are proving too much for them. They do not merely release their own head of steam, which they might do by throwing plates at the wall; they receive supportive power from us.

I think that is what we are doing in serious prayer of intercession: we are entering into and adding our charge to a pervasive spiritual force. And we can only do it by first sensitizing and involving ourselves when we are concerned, not only with those who hurl themselves personally into our time and space, but with unknown persons lingering half a lifetime in prisons with whom we can establish a bond. I believe our serious prayers strengthen and heal them. And if we pray for the oppressors and the unjust, and for those who are aggressive because they are full of hate and fear, then I believe in the same way that we can enter their hearts and challenge them or soften them or open out their closedness. I do not understand the workings of pervasive spiritual force or life-force, but it seems possible to give it particular directions by our own conscious acts. It seems to me to be connected with all kinds of phenomena – divining, parapsychology, crowd psychology, spiritual healing, even ghosts. As to ghosts, there seems to be evidence that both regular human habits and violent human emotion can leave something like 'traces' on a physical space, which others coming along later can pick up even in such a way that the traces can translate themselves back again into visual experience.

What has all this to do with God, and therefore with prayer? If this sort of force or power operates, is it not a purely natural force? Well, in the light of all that was said above about the grace of Christ, you can probably see the sort of answer I would give. I do not think there is a purely natural order, on which the grace of Christ is superimposed; I do not think there is such a thing as 'a purely natural force'. I do not think God is just transcendent (out there) or just immanent (down under). I think he is immanent in our human world, and therefore in us, in a transcendent way: he is involved, but it is he – God – who is involved and to be encountered in our outer human world and in our inner experience. If God addresses, gives himself in his own being, to every man and woman at the roots of their experience, then he ultimately *is* the Spirit-force out of which comes all life; and his Spirit holds all men and women, and in some sense all life and all creation, together in one. So prayer for others goes to the source of their life.

We need 'models' or paradigms, and there is one, not the only one and not necessarily the best one, that may help us. We lived for a long time with a mechanical picture of the world: the world as a vast machine, with many intricate interlocking parts, a network of causes and effects; eternally functioning the same way, so that increased knowledge meant discovering the exact nature and cause-effect relations of the smallest components, so that we could control it all better. (Good old superman – that has meaning and reality which leads to control!) The model enabled enormous advances in the natural sciences to take place, and it may well still be the pervasive model in many people's minds (long after the natural sciences have abandoned it). They may even think it is the only possible model. It makes God somewhat redundant except, possibly, as an originator of the whole outfit; he cannot decently be thought of as intervening and interrupting the beautifully intricate machine; he might have something in store for us at the end of life; but by and large he is 'not wanted on the voyage'. The defects of the model have become increasingly obvious: it never had much place for beauty and moral goodness, for music, for poetry, for art, for creative imagination, for love, in other words for all that is most human about human beings; medicine almost had to be 'physical medicine'; and love between persons was in danger of being dissolved without remainder into chemistry and psychic urges. So we need another model, which no doubt has its own defects. The sciences themselves provide one, as indeed they always have provided models for understanding the structure of reality, sometimes called metaphysics. It is observed that at the level of physics anomalies or surds occur, which cannot be accounted for at that level of system but only at a higher one. So, again, at the levels of inorganic and organic chemistry, where the surds of physics can be resolved. The biological system copes with the anomalies of the lower-level systems, but produces its own. So we move up to the human sciences, through something like envelopes of systems, each of which seems to control the system below it. The human being is a 'system' and can, for instance, direct the undamaged part of the brain after a stroke or accident to take over the functions of a damaged part, to a greater or lesser extent. Then there is society, and we are beginning to understand the degree to which society acts as one and controls the behaviour of individual men and women. Could we perhaps think of God as the system who/that controls all systems? Fanciful? Yes, but not more than other models, and you could do worse; and finding the best available model is the way discoveries are made: it opens the way to truth and understanding.

Words, words, words

On joining the noviceship we were all taught about meditation and mental prayer in its various forms. We came to learn that thinking thoughts about Christian life and doctrine, and putting them into words, was more of a preparatory process or process of assimilation, than prayer itself. Prayer was the resultant state, the grasp of God and resolution about action, that these processes brought about. We soon came to realize (and some who could not think thoughts in time of prayer did so from the beginning) that prayer was more a matter of the heart than of the mind; affective; a giving of the whole self in a single, simple act. After very few years of meditation, times of prayer became an attempt at simply 'being with God', and any techniques could only serve to put us there and keep us there, wordlessly. The development of understanding took place at other times and by other means.

And then came the Divine Office, the private recitation of the breviary which took about fifty minutes each day.

When the disciples asked Jesus to teach them how to pray, he gave them the 'Our Father'. There are two versions in the gospels, the shorter in Luke and the longer in Matthew. Scholarly study has shown that the original was in very simple rhyming couplets, two words to the line: something like, 'Father: blest thy name, come thy reign. . . . ' Luke's version is nearer to the original. The point really is the simplicity and brevity of the prayer, rather than its content: the short invocations can be paralleled elsewhere in Jewish literature; but each phrase takes new meaning for a Christian. The emphasis falls specially on 'thy kingdom come', because any Jew, then or now, in referring to God says 'Blessed be He', a parenthesis. So what Jesus said was: 'When you pray say: "Father (blest be thy name), thy kingdom come."' The irony is that it is in Matthew's gospel that Jesus introduces the prayer by saying, 'When you pray, don't babble on like the pagans (don't rabbit on), but simply say. . . . ' (Matt. 6.7) And yet it is precisely Matthew who shows that the church has started adding glosses to the originally simple rhythms: '(Our) Father (who art in heaven), hallowed be thy name: thy kingdom come (i.e. thy will be done on earth as it is in heaven). . . . ' People are irresistibly tempted to add bits, to say more, to add beautiful thoughts, to explain, to make sure everything is covered and that God and mankind are both fully informed. And the church invented the Divine Office.

Little of what I have to say has any bearing on the choral singing of the Office in a monastic community. I am speaking of the obligation on priests who have not got a contemplative vocation to private recitation of the Divine Office daily. It was in Latin for the first eighteen years or so of my life as a priest. And though I understood Latin a great deal better than most priests owing to advantages of school and university education, I found it a dreadful burden. My own mind carried on quite happily with its thoughts, distractions, in English, while my eye coursed over the pages of the breviary, and it was impossibly difficult to force my attention down to what I was muttering. It was beyond the resources of my will-power to perform the task at a measured pace, extracting meaning from the page: the temptation to squeeze in Matins or Terce, when you had twenty or five minutes to spare before the next bell rang, was irresistible; otherwise in a very busy day you reached bedtime with either forty minutes 'praying' to do, or bed and a bad conscience. How often I found myself saying, 'What a joy it would be just to pray peacefully in my own way for half an hour, if only I didn't have to say my Office.' The Office put an end to any development or perseverance I might have had in mental prayer, in 'being with God'. I wonder what he made of all the efforts of those years? I recaptured something of 'real prayer' in times of annual retreat and felt sure that this was how it was meant to be for the rest of the year: the illusion that one could 'with greater effort' preserve in the midst of the unremitting battering of daily commitments something of the tranquil 'being with God' that returned during times of retreat. Try harder next year. If only I didn't have to 'say the Office'. I think God must have a sense of humour over these antics. It was singularly lacking in me.

Then there is the content of the Office. It is mostly Psalms: there used to be more of them, and they were unexpurgated. I lacked the spiritual sense of some of my brethren, who could tune in sweetly and serenely to the primordial passions of Middle Eastern men, sounding off before God about the vileness of other men relishing the slaughter of their enemies and the dogs licking up their blood, nationalism, jingoism, vindictiveness. . . . It took too much effort to transpose it all into an allegorical key and pray in a Christian way about the evils that threaten humanity. I was not brought up with Bible stories at my mother's knee, stories of which I had grown fond. I found many rather repulsive and many more a very tedious repetition year after year. I often found myself thinking how pleasant it would be to pray from Christian literature. Of course there are 'nice bits' and great bits in the Old Testament, including the Psalms, but they do not make up a high proportion of the whole. Of course you need to grasp the main religious concepts of Israel and trace their development, if you are to understand the forms in which New Testament writers express their Christian faith; but you don't have to do that in a time of prayer – in fact much better not. The whole thing posed an intellectual and religious problem, disruptive of prayer. There was enormous pressure to regard the Bible (any part of it) as simply 'the word of God', totally different in kind from any other Christian or religious literature. And yet how *could* much of it be regarded as 'God speaking' and what sort of God spoke thus? The problem remained, as a burden of conscience, until I came to realize (as I have briefly indicated above) that God inspires people, and people's expression of their awareness of God in life owes much to their own present human horizons and development.

I was about sixty and had tried to keep up with the Office

for twenty-five years, in English for the last ten or so, when I was liberated from it. This happened to me at a workshop run for Jesuits by a very free spirit, Tony de Mello. The course he gave us on techniques in prayer drawn from the experience of eastern religions is included in his book *Sadhana*.[1] He was not expressly talking about the Office, but his personality and freedom of approach to various ways of praying, including the integration in prayer of the body and the imagination, made a great light of common sense burst forth in my mind. I cannot think why it had not done so a great deal earlier, as it probably did with many of my contemporaries. Henceforth, I resolved, I would use the breviary if and when and to the extent that it helped me to pray. If three sentences, or one, put me in touch with God, I would stay there and let the rest of the day's Office go by the board. Or I would use other texts and perhaps not open my breviary for a month or more. (I did do quite a lot of reading about scripture at other times.) In a sense my efforts at prayer picked up from where they had got to twenty-five years before.

It may cause difficulties to some that I thus dispensed myself from daily recitation of the Office, an obligation I had undertaken. This raises questions about the nature of such obligations, about the place of church rules in one's relationship with God, and more broadly about the law and the gospel, which are too large to tackle here. I will only say that I now find the Office a gift for prayer, whereas for long years it was a barrier.

On being turned round

Then more recently, something else happened. I was firmly turned round to face the other way.

It did not happen suddenly but gradually over a period of about a month. It followed on a fairly long period not so much of dryness and lack of savour as of complete deadness of feeling, in which I could not say I had any faith at all, or that religious ideas and imagery had the slightest meaning. It came about by reading the books of the Carmelite prioress, Ruth Burrows. Again, it was not so much the direct content of her

[1] de Mello, *Sadhana*, Institute of Jesuit Resources, USA.

writing but an underlying current that did the trick. I did not feel that the 'three islands' in her *Guidelines to Mystical Prayer*[2] had very much bearing on my sort of life and vocation, or corresponded to anything much in my experience, even while I found her exposition of stages in mystical contemplation fascinating, clearing away as it did a lot of confusion and even lumber. What came through to me was a profound conviction, or awareness rather than conviction, of the priority of the action of God at all points. One sentence struck me with particular force, a very simple sentence: 'God unites his being with mine.' *God* does it, not I.

When I say I was turned round to face the other way, I mean that 'I was turned' rather than that I decided to turn. By 'facing the other way' I mean the following. All efforts at praying had been efforts of mine, using various ways and means, to find God, to be aware of God, to discern God – whether those earlier meditations or thinking-out processes; or later attitudes of simply looking or regarding, often of peering perhaps unsuccessfully into the haze; or just techniques of posture, of breathing, of repeating phrases, in order to become subliminally aware of God both 'out there' and 'in here'. St Ignatius of Loyola often wrote in his letters to his followers that they should not only find God in their times of prayer but that they should seek (or find) him in all things, in all events, all day. The suggestion is that the activity should be ours. Now all of a sudden God was giving himself to me in everything in life, coming at me from all corners of the room one might say. Everything was gift: the warmth or cold the sunshine or rain, the beauty or the ordinariness. Particularly were all the people that I met 'gift'. I did not have to go looking, as if God was somewhere to be found hidden away behind reality. I had only to receive, to welcome, to accept, to be aware. He was giving himself to me in all reality. I could be aware of this anywhere, at any time of day, but it seemed particularly urgent, necessary, to set aside some times when I could simply 'be' in his presence and let him 'unite his being with mine'. If I picked up the dear old Office (or any other book of prayer) God 'came at' me in certain phrases: not the ones that were all about what

[2]Ruth Burrows, *Guidelines to Mystical Prayer*, Sheed and Ward 1976.

we/I wanted or were doing or hoping, but the sentences about God's action. Not 'O Lord, listen to my prayer and let my cry for help reach you'; but, 'O Lord, you search me and you know me, you know my resting and my rising, you discern my purpose from afar'. Not 'They are happy whose life is blameless, who follow God's law'; but 'The Lord's right hand has triumphed; his right hand raised me up', and 'This day was made by the Lord; we rejoice and are glad.' And so with liturgical texts, as I have said of eucharistic belief: not, 'we offer the eternal sacrifice of Christ', but 'he gathers us into his eternal self- offering'.

Finally, what about Jesus? Edward Schillebeeckx has written perceptively about two very different styles of Christianity, the Jesus-style and the Christ-style,[3] with their high and low interest in the man Jesus, the church, social and political engagement, evangelization and conversion. At the same time, many of Christian background have difficulties about a 'personal' God and are more at home in believing in Life, the Absolute, the All, etc. The Carmelite writers, Teresa and John of the Cross, wrestle with the problem of the abstraction of their language about the God experienced in contemplative prayer, and the centrality of Jesus Christ in the devotion of Christians. I have once or twice preached a sermon poking fun at the intellectual antics of some modern theologians by taking the Caesarea Philippi story and changing it into modern dress: Jesus asked Peter, 'Who do men say that I am?'; Peter scratched his head and replied, 'Well, some say you are the ground of their being; others, the thou at the heart of every I-thou encounter; others say absolute process; others, the pervasive life-force; others, the system who controls all systems'; and Jesus wept.

It really would be very strange for a *Christian* to have any profound problem about the personal nature of God, or how to express God in human terms. The wisdom of God was made flesh (our sort of man) and dwelt amongst us. He gave himself definitive self-expression in human terms and does not need any other. Jesus personalizes God for me, once and for all. That being said, and not forgotten – that being said, and still

[3]E. Schillebeeckx, *Jesus: An Experiment in Christology*, Collins 1978, pp. 29–30.

leaving room for all sorts of patterns of understanding the relation of the mortal Jesus and the risen Jesus to the God whom from within his Jewish faith he called 'Father' – there is of course room for conceptual patterns galore to explore, but not to replace or to translate without remainder the concrete self-gift of God in history. Two things seem to me quite wrong-headed: either to replace Jesus of Nazareth by conceptual images; or to choose between the crucified-one and the crucified-and-risen-one; between Jesus and Christ. It is not a question of choosing between the Jesus of history and the rather more diffuse Christ of faith. It was Jesus who rose and *became* Lord and Christ (Acts 2.36); and both are objects of faith.[4] The Jesus of history has got to be unearthed from the God in human clothes (often a nightdress) of much Christian devotion. The Jesus of history is in many ways a craggy and awkward figure for assimilation into white liberal bourgeois consumer society, though perhaps not so out of place in India or Central America. The Jesus of history grew in wisdom and in stature and in favour with God and man (Luke 2.52) and was not at all points in his life and in his sayings totally comprehending of God and man or of his own role in God's plan of self-giving. In any case, we only have him filtered through faith in Jesus the Lord, the Christ, the faith of those who themselves belonged totally in a place, a time, a horizon, and filtered him through the perceptions available to them. There are no ways of resolving the questions to which all this gives rise. The point, rather, is that they are not to be resolved: we have to live today with today's faith, in today's world, always challenged by the faith-picture of those who first believed in the risen Christ present by his Spirit and still active among them. There are unanswerable puzzles about this real human person, the risen Lord Jesus Christ, in his individual reality, filled with God's Spirit in whom he encounters and invades us: should he be thought of as a Jew? As wholly masculine? etc. But the traditional doctrine of the Trinity, for all its limitations, should at least teach us that personhood in God is not a cut-off-ness but a giving-to and a dwelling-in the reality of the other. And so there is really no problem about

[4]I have written more fully on this in *Faith in Jesus Christ*, Darton, Longman and Todd 1980.

how the God and Father of our Lord Jesus Christ is personal for me today. He is personal in all the persons in whom he addresses and encounters me, gives himself to me, unites his being with mine, and so reconciles men and women with each other, and all with him.